Elizabeth

with

CW00506012

for 18ᵗʰ May 1985

SELECTED POEMS

EDMUND BLUNDEN

Selected Poems
edited by Robyn Marsack

CARCANET NEW PRESS / MANCHESTER

First published in Great Britain in 1982 by
Carcanet New Press Limited
330 Corn Exchange Buildings
Manchester M4 3BG

British Library Cataloguing in Publication Data
Blunden, Edmund
    Selected Poems.
    I. Title   II. Marsack, Robyn
    821'.912   PR6003.L8

ISBN 0-85635-425-2

*The publisher acknowledges the financial assistance of the Arts Council of
Great Britain.*

Printed in England by Short Run Press Ltd., Exeter.

CONTENTS

All poems are printed as they first appeared in collected form; asterisks indicate either a departure from that rule or a title later altered by Blunden, explained in the notes.

INTRODUCTION

'A POET who once gets marked by the reviewers with the ranch-brand of the anthology in which he first appears is thereafter made to suffer for the failings of the other weaker members of the herd,' Robert Graves wrote to the *Times Literary Supplement* (1 December 1921). Precisely this problem has dogged Edmund Blunden, who like Graves was one of Edward Marsh's 'Georgians'. Although associated chiefly with *The Athenaeum* and thus firmly in the literary centre—Squire's *London Mercury* energetically on the right, *Art and Letters* adventurously to the left—Blunden also published his poems in more experimental little magazines such as *Coterie*, which featured Huxley and Gaudier-Brzeska. Nevertheless, the reception of his poetry has been shadowed by the hostility that greeted *Georgian Poetry 1920-1921* as the purveyor of an outworn style. (1)

After the enormous popularity of volumes I and II, the third of the series varied its accepted themes with the admission of harsher war poetry by Sassoon and Graves. By the fourth anthology, the insubstantial escapism of poets such as John Freeman had won the ascendancy. In his critical assessment *The Georgian Revolt* (1967), Robert Ross concludes: 'In 1912 and 1915 "Georgian" had implied vigour, revolt and youth. After 1917 it was to imply retrenchment, escape and enervation' (p. 187). At a time when *The Criterion*'s first issue carried *The Waste Land*, the publication of *Georgian Poetry* V demonstrated just how far Marsh's editorial perception was inadequate to post-war circumstances. Certain contemporary reviewers did make an exception of Blunden in their dismissal of the 'rainbows, cuckoos, daffodils and timid hares'-school (Eliot, *The Egoist*, March 1918), but in praising his gift for rural observation failed to distinguish that quality in his poetry at odds with Middleton Murry's complaint in *The Athenaeum* (5 December 1919), 'there is nothing disturbing' about the Georgians.

Blunden was aware of the stereotyping from which he suffered, and protested mildly in the preface to *The Poems* (1930): 'The titles and contents of my books "The Waggoner" and "The Shepherd" have, I apprehend, done me a slight injustice; that is, they have labelled me among the poets of the time as a useful rustic ... Great as is the power of country life over me, and of that stately march of the seasons...yet I have always suspected myself of some inclination to explore other subjects.'

If the chief weakness of Georgian poetry was pseudo-pastoralism, allegiance to a specifically English tradition of nature poetry was in

Mention of any poem included in the selection will be followed by its page number.

Blunden's case a source of strength. He derived his understated authority from the fact that rural subjects were for him inseparable from childhood, whose intense pleasures and fears he described in an essay in Simon Nowell-Smith's compilation, *Edwardian England* (1964). Blunden's boyhood was spent in Yalding, Kent: 'it was hardly possible for any of us not to know something of our three rivers, each differing in character, of our hopfields and orchards and sheepfolds, and much else that was apparently eternal. If I wrote eagerly of these things it was not because I was following . . . "The Georgians" . . . but because my themes were daily experiences' (*Poetry Book Society Bulletin*, no. 14). These were enlarged when Blunden attended Christ's Hospital, which had recently moved from London to Horsham, in the middle of the Sussex Weald. Blunden was passionately attached to the school and its literary traditions, proud of sharing with Coleridge the title of Senior Grecian, i.e. head of the school.

In 1916, when he should have been a freshman at Oxford and was instead in a military training camp, four small, privately printed collections of Blunden's poetry were published. He declared his literary loyalties in the dedication of *The Barn* to Leigh Hunt (another Old Blue) and of *Three Poems* to John Clare; his regional ones in the preamble to *Pastorals*: 'I sing of the rivers and hamlets and woodlands of Sussex and Kent'. 'The Barn' eventually initiated an important friendship when Blunden, hoping for a notice in the literary columns of the *Daily Herald*, sent it to Siegfried Sassoon. Sassoon felt he had 'discovered a poet': '. . . for the barn was physically evoked, with its cobwebs and dust and sparkling sun, its smell of cattle-cake and apples stored in hay . . . description of mill-wheel and weir, beautifully exact . . . where authentic fishes basked' (*Siegfried's Journey*, 1945, p. 146). While affectionately precise description is its mainstay, the poem is also the narrative of a supernatural visitation that has disastrous consequences for the farm until the curse is laboriously banished. The material is handled uneconomically, and in later poems he refrained from drawing such explicit morals, but Blunden conveys his regard for the spirit of place, his intuitions of unease, a sense of lurking malignity. In this he resembles Walter de la Mare, whom he admired.

Blunden's reaction to his war service took its special bias—that of the 'harmless young shepherd in a soldier's coat'—from the double inheritance of his country upbringing and an already extensive knowledge of literature, of the mid-eighteenth to early nineteenth centuries in particular. To these was joined the traditional classical training of a public schoolboy, shared with many officers. It was, as Paul Fussell has demonstrated in *The Great War and Modern Memory* (1975), a very 'literary war'.

Nature and agriculture provided Blunden with the norms of health; literature, in the form of Clare's poems or Edward Young's exclamatory *Night Thoughts* ('*Helpless* Immortal! Insect *infinite*!'), established some kind of continuity with a life once known, or with that of previous generations. These furnished perspectives from which to cope with immediate horrors, in trenches where each man developed his own strategy of self-preservation. Fussell is right to say that in *Undertones of War* (1928), as in the poetry, Blunden took great risks with his 'arcadian recourses' (see *The Great War*, Chapter VII). He does not always avoid the traps of sentimentality and prettiness: in the war poems, however, these failings are rare. 'The Unchangeable' (1917, *The Waggoner*), with its stubborn pleasure in nature, characteristically combines irony, literary allusiveness, verbal precision and skilful cadence:

> Though I within these two last years of grace
> Have seen the bright Ancre scourged to brackish mire,
> And meagre Belgian becks by dale and chace
> Stamped into sloughs of death with battering fire—
> Spite of all this, I sing you high and low,
> My old loves, Waters, be you shoal or deep,
> Waters whose lazy and continual flow
> Learns at the drizzling weir the tongue of sleep.

It is not simply a matter of ironic contrasts, though they are made, or of judging that the old conventions are entirely inadequate to the new situation. Value resides in the language itself. Invoking traditional patterns in descriptions of trench warfare measured not only Blunden's loss of innocence but a whole society's loss, more immediately devastating than industrial and suburban encroachment. For a night in 1916, Blunden was housed in a farm cottage: 'Peaceful little one, standest thou yet? cool nook, earthly paradisal cupboard with leaf-green light to see poetry by, I fear much that 1918 was the ruin of thee' (*Undertones*, Penguin, p. 74). This style of archaism, apostrophe, rhetorical questioning, and the personifications scattered throughout the text—Love, Fancy, Detraction—are not decorative, they are essential to his meaning. There has been a time when such diction, like precisely planned gardens and efficient husbandry, was a standard, part of an ideally harmonious, intellectually sanctioned order. For Blunden pastoralism was not an empty academic form, it recreated the natural world he had intimately known.

The subtle interpenetration of human, non-human, and inanimate objects is one of the strengths of Blunden's war poetry. The materials of war are treacherously naturalised, as in the concluding stanza of 'A House in Festubert' (*Undertones*):

> It hived the bird's call, the bee's hum,
> The sunbeams crossing the garden's shade—
> So fond of summer! still they come,
> But steel-born bees, birds, beams invade.
> —Could summer betray you?

The juxtaposition of flowers and war, both telling and banal in Great War literature, is brilliantly used by Blunden in 'Vlamertinghe: Passing the Chateau, July 1917' (p. 60). The title, as Jon Silkin remarks in *Out of Battle* (1972, p. 110), would be appropriate to some leisurely diary of a grand tour: here the soldiers' experience and a literary rendition are at odds. 'Ode on a Grecian Urn' furnishes the opening line: Blunden's poem answers the question raised in stanza four, 'Who are these coming to the sacrifice?' Keats's wondering spectator composes an origin for the sacrificial procession, sees a town deserted in the stasis of art: 'and not a soul to tell/Why thou art desolate, can e'er return'. It might end so for the troops going up the line, prematurely, incongruously amidst flowers, offering their own reproof to fact and to the poetry dressing it as 'damask' and 'vermilion'. Do truth and beauty coincide, or are they at war in such a scene?

As the war continued, especially after the terrible attack on Hamel and the action of Passchendaele—when Blunden's battalion suffered about 275 casualties in three days—nature's restorative power began to weaken: 'the grimness of war began to compete as a subject with the pastorals of peace. By the end of [1916], when madness seemed totally to rule the hour, I was almost a poet of the shell-holes, of ruin and of mortification' (*War Poets 1914-1918*, 1958, p. 24). In *Undertones of War*, the occurrence of leaves spent in England is merely noted: it is as though the only reality lay in France. 'Reunion in War' (*The Shepherd*) makes it plain that human relations, outside those with fellow soldiers, could not touch a man:

> We had not met but a moment ere
>   War baffled joy, and cried,
> 'Love's but a madness, a burnt flare;
>   The shell's a madman's bride.'

It is dead men's bones that the lover envies. Blunden later expressed his own sense of guilt at having survived, 'And knew for all my fear to die/ That I with those lost friends should lie' ('War Autobiography', *The Shepherd*). One of the epigraphs he chose for his memoir was 'Yea, how they set themselves in battle-array/I shall remember to my dying day'. The memoir is concerned with the battalion's experiences rather than Blunden's. Indications of his personality as it appeared to others are rare: his colonel says, 'Rabbit, they're short of ammunition' and we are given a notion of the impression he produced. There is, typically, no mention of his earning the Military Cross. 'Another Journey from Bethune to Cuinchy' (*Undertones*) refers to the repeated treks of 1916 and to the poet's emotional need to 'go over the ground again', but in its zig-zag of identity between soldier and civilian, Blunden cannot ascertain his position. The year before his death he chose 'Can You Remember?' (p. 86) to represent his work in an anthology, because 'my experiences in the First World War have haunted me all my life and for many days I have, it seemed, lived in that world rather than this' (*Let the Poet Choose*, ed. James Gibson, 1973, p. 31).

This sense of displacement prevails in the poems of the immediate post-war. Ghosts form in battalions between Blunden and his new, married life. French scenes intervene when he walks the English country, 'The very bat that stoops and whips askance/Shrills malice at the soul grown strange in France' ('The Estrangement', 1919, *The Waggoner*). '1916 Seen from 1921' (p. 32), which Sassoon thought Blunden's finest war poem, displays both an alienation from the present and an attraction to the dazzling fertility of natural phenomena in the trenches. The 'green places here' fail to stay the imagination, which goes out to the flood of 'self-sown wheat', the roses and lizards in the redoubt. The green of trees at Hamel is more immediate to him, memory more vivid, than actuality. The paradoxes are painful to live with, though later Blunden is able to distil the original peace of his childhood surroundings in 'Old Homes' (*The Shepherd*). There he maintains that 'Beyond estranging years that cloaked my view/With all their wintriness of fear and strain;/I turned to you, I never turned in vain', concluding, 'in your pastoral still my life has rest'. The vision serves him as 'A herb of grace to keep the will from madding'.

Elements of insecurity are evident in the way other poems are honeycombed with martial vocabulary and meaning long after the war. 'The Pike' (p. 18) is a well-known example: the weir has 'bastions' and its apparent peace is destroyed by the fish's sudden murderous offensive. The wind in 'Spring Night' (p. 27) blows "So mad . . . so truceless and so grim,/As if day's host of flowers were a moment's whim'. 'Host', an entirely familiar metaphor, would go unnoticed except that the striking 'truceless' alerts us to its original context, in which men's lives as brief as flowers are subject to the scythe. The lines demonstrate Blunden's

5

talent for fine endings. In 'Perch-Fishing' (p. 23) a boy's angling skills, the catch of the 'ogling hunchbacked perch with needled fin', are eclipsed by Blunden's transfer of sympathy to the bereft mate, thinking of 'a thousand things the whole year through/They did together, never more to do'. The human lament for comrades slain is palpable, the usurping agony persists.

1919 emerges from the poems as a year of dread and foreboding. Blunden was established in Oxford, but not very happily. Graves has left a wry account of the way military reflexes interfered with their attempts to follow lectures (*Goodbye to All That*, 1957, Chapter 27). He encouraged Blunden to send work to Edward Marsh, and the dispatch of *The Harbingers* in September resulted in another friendship. Blunden wrote despondently that after his youthful facility, 'Poetry is now to me a most difficult and laborious affair, and I begin to wonder whether I have any poetry in me. . . . If I lived in Kent, I should write good poems in bundles of ten'. Marsh was enthusiastic; with his usual tact and generosity he gave Blunden some of the proceeds from his memoir of Rupert Brooke. Not long afterwards Graves reported that 'Blunden is beginning to write in a magnificently competent way. You should see "Almswomen". It makes me cry every time' (quoted by Christopher Hassall, *Edward Marsh: Patron of the Arts*, 1959, pp. 470-71).

The aftertones of war were deepened by a personal tragedy for Blunden, the death in 1919 of his daughter Joy, aged forty days. The first poem about a spring visit to her grave seems to find consolation in the nature that recalls her; the simple poignancy of 'To Joy' (p. 70) makes a deeper impression. With 'In a Country Churchyard' (p. 54, published in June 1925), religious and pantheistic comfort has receded. With desperation, he sees death as change, motion; the formal stanzaic pattern, like the deceptively unyielding church tower, loses its hold over emotion:

> So lies thy skull? This earth, even this
> Like quicksand weaves.
> Sleep well, my darling, though I kiss
> Lime or dead leaves.

Ample use was made of quick-lime in the trenches to hasten decomposition and conceal the stench: in 'even this' Blunden implies a similarity between the churchyard and the burial grounds he knew. The poem subjects all creation to the same 'deadly flowing'.

Unable to adapt to academic life, Blunden moved to London to work on *The Athenaeum*, then *The Nation*. He was awarded the Hawthornden Prize in 1922 for his collection *The Shepherd*, recognition of his reputation as a poet. The next year he sailed for Tokyo, to take up a position as Professor of English at the Imperial University. He was to return to Japan after World War II as a Cultural Liaison Officer, when he travelled throughout the country, increasing the affection and respect he had gained in his first stay. Blunden found much that was sympathetic in the 'beautiful and dexterous and delicate detail of existence' in Japanese art ('Line Upon Line', *The Mind's Eye*, p. 112), in the modesty and courtesy of his pupils, and the tranquil austerity of the sacred places shown to him. 'A Japanese Evening' (p. 70) hints at the barriers to understanding, while it registers a discreetly sensuous awareness of another culture. Asked what influence these two periods exerted on his work, Blunden replied: 'I think that living in Japan made a difference even in one's handwriting and perhaps in one's manner . . . . I'm sure my whole style of thought has been touched by Japanese experiences. For the poetry part, I suspect I cut the corners a little finer than I used to do' (*The Poet Speaks*, ed. Peter Orr, 1966, p. 34). That was not apparent in the poems of the 1930s, when he had returned to England and after a time to Oxford, as Fellow and Tutor in English at Merton College.

Having subdued his ghosts by writing *Undertones of War* in Tokyo Blunden could turn to repaying debts of gratitude to the literature that had helped sustain him. That to John Clare he had acknowledged when first at Oxford by painstaking work on manuscripts, indeed beginning the Clare revival, and he continued to edit and write about the poet. A judgement in the preface to *Poems Chiefly from Manuscript* suggests affinities between them, besides their shared precision of observation and a faith—sternly tried in both men—in a universal order. Blunden remarks that 'imagination, colour, melody and affection were Clare's by nature,' but 'sometimes his incredible facility in verse . . . was not his best friend'. Meditations on the poetry led Blunden to write 'The Death Mask of John Clare' (*Masks of Time*), which despite its evocation of the asylum is resolutely serene, and its antithesis, 'Clare's Ghost' (p. 25). Peace is pitched out, the wild night calls up and images all the restlessly uncompromising aspects of genius. He was also to make major contributions to knowledge of the Romantics, especially of Shelley. 'The Wartons and Other Early Romantics' drew an appreciative poem, as did the lesser landscape artists in 'A Favourite Scene: recalled on looking at Birket Foster's landscapes'.

Blunden's interests were by no means confined to the eighteenth and nineteenth centuries. Milton had first revealed the excitement of poetry to him, and he nearly always carried a small copy of *Paradise Lost*. Blunden had an unreserved admiration for Vaughan—on whom he wrote

7

a short book—Herbert, and Marvell. 'The Garden' and Collins's 'Ode to Evening' were perhaps his favourite poems. He had a clear conception of the English poetic tradition, liked owning to poetic ancestors and sought to connect the generations. His schoolboy apprenticeship was to Coleridge, whose work finds echoes in Blunden's to the very last. Coleridge himself was 'deep in the verse of Collins', as Blunden pointed out in the introduction to his edition of Collins's poems in 1929. All three poets are attracted to the supernatural. Blunden describes Collins as 'a bell calling his many poetic disciples into a region unvisited by the shocks of events and the injuries of society' (p. 36). Such regions were created by Blunden, who summoned the gods and shades of Augustan poetry to inhabit them. It is Blunden's ability to suggest the unsettling through conventional means that his more successful poems share with Collins's: 'his art has caught the mystery in the circumstances of every day, making us freshly conceive the truth of fairy fancy'. Blunden found 'How Sleep the Brave' 'the most consoling and unstrained elegy for our dead in Flanders'; he did not attempt analysis, having learned to love the poem 'under conditions which have tested poetic preference with searching and tyrannous insistency' (p. 38).

Along with the creation of mood and setting, the essence of Blunden's criticism is appreciation. Theoretical controversies or the ranking of poets held no interest for him. He wrote often of the pleasures of book-collecting, his own resulting in a fine personal library and a donation of books to Keats House, Hampstead. His flair for rescuing first editions from unpromising book-barrows is paralleled by his sympathetic ability to locate modest achievements, as in his 'Wayside' anthologies. Blunden had a discerning eye for the work of his distinguished war contemporaries, producing an influential edition of Wilfrid Owen's poems in 1931, and in an effort to save Ivor Gurney's poetry from neglect, edited his *Poems* (mainly from unpublished manuscripts) in 1954.

Blunden's reputation as a poet declined in the 1930s. Michael Roberts, whose anthology virtually shaped the taste of a generation, excluded him from *The Faber Book of Modern Verse* in 1936 as one of those who had written good poems but had not 'been compelled to make any notable development of poetic technique' (Introduction, p. 1). In *New Bearings in English Poetry* (1932), F. R. Leavis had dealt with this point in praising Blunden's distinctive poise: 'He was able to be, to some purpose, conservative in technique and to draw upon the eighteenth century, because the immemorial rural order that was doomed is real to him'. Leavis however censured Blunden's more recent poetry for being on the one hand too hospitable to 'nymphs and their attendant classicalities' and on the other too directly descriptive of 'his unease, his inner tensions, instead of implying them, as before, in the solidity of his created world' (Penguin ed., pp. 53-4). These criticisms are not unjustified of the volumes after *Undertones of War*, when Blunden showed a tendency to be too indulgent towards his familiar themes. That he also realised the pitfalls of his approach is evident in 'The Sunlit Vale' (p. 73), which admits the charm of eighteenth-century diction, and of innocent perception, at the same time criticising them as ultimately untenable fancies. The poem elicits an unsettling and mysterious recognition of the forces behind natural beauty: the scene, and the poet celebrating it, 'fail, though you smile—/That other does not smile'. Direct, it is not without subtlety.

This scepticism concerning nature's benevolence allies Blunden with Thomas Hardy, as does the tone, metre and stanzaic form of a number of poems; for instance 'Familiarity' (p. 63), where Blunden plays with and rejects the tricks of appearance. Graves, Sassoon and Blunden each visited Hardy in the 1920s and his emphasis on the traditional craft of poetry, his reaction against modernism, was influential with them all (see Blunden's brief notes on his conversations with Hardy in Hopkins's selection). Blunden closes *Undertones of War* with 'Return of the Native', dated Ypres 1929, written after one of his many returns to the battle-sites. He exploits Hardy's title to indicate the extent of his exile from ordinary life, the impossibility of constructing a less costly relationship with the past that obsesses him, and nature's cool reassertion over ground whose every inch had been contested:

> Leaving us with this south-west breeze to whisper
> In bushes younger than the brows it cooled
> Foreheads still trenched with feverish wonderings
> Of what was once Time's vast compulsion, now
> Incapable to stir a weed or moth.

Whereas he knew that the close rural communities had been broken up—like Hardy he had acknowledged their faults and constrictions—and that the countryside was being despoiled, Blunden's disenchantments were less corrosive than Hardy's. Unlike Hardy, he possessed a quiet religious faith. There were times when that failed, or at least profoundly mystified Blunden; he writes of 'God's freezing love', turns the Psalmist's certainty upside-down at the beginning of 'Report on Experience' and ends the poem ambiguously, 'Over there are faith, life, virtue in the sun' (p. 67). It is distant, a curious proof, a far country. How often Blunden uses 'gilded' in *Undertones of War* for the deceptive action of the sun setting on horrors, shining on barbed wire. Remembering that usage, the close of his 'Report' seems less kindly in its promise. In the 1920s, Blunden passed through a phase of religious awe that left him with a sense of a benevolent Creator—'The splendours of the world/Are such that number and inquiry fade'—although this was challenged by his desire to relate belief to scientific discovery. Since experience with Blunden could rarely be separated from literature, his belief was buttressed by the poetry of Vaughan and Herbert, the prose of Traherne: 'O God that Abraham and our Vaughan knew,/Hide not thyself, let first love prove not wrong' ('A Psalm', *To Nature*).

In *Shells by a Stream* (1944) there was the prospect of a new and happy marriage to celebrate. As though the declaration of war in 1939 had released him from the perturbation of the preceding years, the set pieces and unguarded fluency of the 1930s were succeeded by poems of a sparer form and a more intense lyricism. Natural descriptions tended to lose their questioning accent, however, perhaps because Blunden felt that it was time to assert stability and continuity—qualities also present in his tribute to his favourite game, *Cricket Country*: 'It was a book written in the hope that it would help some whom the damn'd war was holding at a distance'. (2) His help extended beyond this book and the more practical teaching of map-reading to undergraduates. Among the pupils he encouraged and aided was Keith Douglas, whose temperament and poetry were quite different from his own. Blunden was convinced that for all the anguish and waste, 'the fighting man in this as in other wars is at least the only man whom truth really cares to meet'. (3)

The 1950s returned Blunden to the East, this time as Professor of English at the University of Hong Kong. For a man of his essentially English sensibility, these periods of exile must have been a strain, despite the friendships he made. The poems of these years return to youthful memories of Kent and Sussex, as well as ranging over the Asian environment. Detail is less abundant than in earlier poetry. Blunden relishes the antics of flies and birds, 'All tenants of an ancient place,' as Clare wrote; like him Blunden had always been concerned to give ' "every weed and blossom" ' an equality with whatever this world contains' (*Nature in English Literature*, p. 58).

'I remember when writing my nature pieces,' Blunden commented in 1965, 'which I don't write so much now, the sense I had was of *painting* rather than describing. Perhaps it is a fault, but there it is' (*The Poet Speaks*, p. 35). This sense of composing a world implies a criticism of the purely descriptive as naively inadequate to the object, but Blunden was far from insistent in his patterning, accepting even the landscape of war as something given, however outrageously. The poet's personal reticence works to guarantee the poem's truth for the reader. In an earlier note on his work, he stressed that his 'notion of a poem was not that it should be just a transcription from nature, but was in part an experiment in style, a light from the writer's own resources of image and art upon the chosen moment and scene. The term "nature poet" is honourable however limited in use, but it should be taken to imply something like a verbal photographer'. (4)

Throughout his career the technical resources of Blunden's art were manifold, from conversation piece to sonnet, elegy to ballad; lyrics extending from the double-accented metrical simplicity of 'The Puzzle' (p. 53) to the intricate modulations of 'Late Light' (p. 84). His poetry was invigorated by the use of dialect words: 'Across the sandy paths the tiny frogs/Go yerking' ('Gods of the Earth Beneath', *The Harbingers*); the 'dragonfly that daps' and the 'glinzy ice' ('In Festubert', p. 21). He also made skilful translations: from the French, a handful from the Greek Anthology, from Horace and a number of seventeenth-century Latin poems by English authors. In earlier volumes, Blunden experimented with monologues, catching a ruminative tone, while not achieving the psychological acuity that Robert Frost did. Yet Blunden and Frost have in common a perception of unyielding nature, that repels man's attempts at communion or description.

That the whole range of traditional forms was accessible to and drawn on by Blunden is characteristic of his perception of time: the past, especially 1914-18, was as actual to him as the present, and this blurring of categories made him a particularly uncontemporary poet. His response to the major international crises engaging his fellow poets was determined by his *ancien combattant*'s mentality. He welcomed the Munich settlement as a means of averting another slaughter; when asked to take sides over the Vietnam war in 1967, Blunden declared his opposition. He liked Clare's motto, taken from Spenser, 'I pipe to please myself'. After 1939 the discountenancing of time is very noticeable in his poetry, as is the increase in metaphysical speculation, never sinewy or visionary, but searching for 'eternal laws'.

'Agree, the way to live/Is not to dissect existence,' Blunden wrote ('In My Time', p. 85). His own poetry is a loving accumulation of detail, a convergence, sometimes disquieting, of spirit and setting.

11

1. The Georgians themselves have been quietly rehabilitated in James Reeves's discriminating Penguin anthology, *Georgian Poetry* (1962), and by Philip Larkin in *The Oxford Book of Twentieth-Century English Verse* (1973).

2. Letter of 19 April 1945 to J. E. Morpurgo, quoted in his tribute 'Edmund Blunden: Poet of Community', *Contemporary Review*, October 1974.

3. Letter to Douglas, quoted by Desmond Graham in *Keith Douglas* (1974), p. 218n. Douglas was another Old Blue, and Blunden wrote to him in 1940: 'We have had some pretty good poets, Peele, Coleridge, Lamb, Hunt, but the line must be extended! and I think you can do it'. Ibid., p. 66.

4. *Poetry Book Society Bulletin*, no. 14. Robert Lowell's poem 'Epilogue' in his last collection, *Day by Day*, shows a similar concern with the modern poet's dilemma between art and photography as working metaphors. Although Lowell is a poet diametrically opposed in effect, two of his lines are reminiscent of Blunden's: *'The painter's vision is not a lens, / it trembles to caress the light.'*

Further Reading

A Bibliography of Edmund Blunden, Brownlee Kirkpatrick, 1979.

Bergonzi, Bernard. *Heroes' Twilight*, 1965, rev. 1980.

Chau, Wah Ching et al, eds. *Edmund Blunden, Sixty-Five*, 1961.

Gardner, Philip. 'Edmund Blunden: War Poet', *University of Toronto Quarterly*, XLII, 1972-3.

Hardie, Alec M. *Edmund Blunden*, 1958, rev. 1971.

Scannell, Vernon. *A Proper Gentleman*, 1977.

Thorpe, Michael. *The Poetry of Edmund Blunden*, 1971.

Willy, Margaret. 'The Poetry of Edmund Blunden', *English*, Autumn 1957.

Acknowledgement

I am most grateful to Edmund Blunden's widow Claire Blunden, to his friend Professor J. E. Morpurgo, and to his biographer Barry Webb for their help and encouragement.

CHRONOLOGY AND SELECT BIBLIOGRAPHY

1896	1 November	Born in London.
1898		Family moves to Yalding, Kent, where the father is a schoolmaster.
1907		Attends Cleave's Grammar School.
1909		Wins scholarship to Christ's Hospital, Horsham. Enters Coleridge 'A' House.
1914		Wins senior classics scholarship at The Queen's College, Oxford.
	October	*Poems 1913 and 1914, Poems Translated from the French*.
		Volunteers and serves with The Southdowns, The Royal Sussex Regiment.
1916	Spring	Having received his commission, goes to France with 11th Royal Sussex. Trench duty at Festubert, Cuinchy, Richebourg.
	May	*The Harbingers*.
	June	*Pastorals*.
	August	Battalion moves to the Somme.
	13 November	Awarded the Military Cross. Battalion at Thiepval.
1917	31 July	Third Ypres offensive (the beginning of Passchendaele).
	October	Gassed (also in July).
1918		Unable to write this year.
	Spring	From Gouzeaucourt returns to a training camp in England.
	June	Marries Mary Daines. There were two daughters and a son of this marriage.
1919	17 February	Demobbed.
	August	Daughter Joy dies.
	October	Takes up place at Oxford.
		Moves to a cottage on Boar's Hill; Masefield and Graves also live there.
1920		Leaves Oxford to become Middleton Murry's assistant on *The Athenaeum*.
	August	*The Waggoner*.
	November	Blunden and Porter's edition of *Poems Chiefly from Manuscript* by John Clare.
1922	April	*The Shepherd and Other Poems of Peace and War*. Receives the Hawthornden Prize.

	December	*The Bonaventure* published, the journal of his voyage earlier in the year in a cargo boat to South America.
1923	November	*Christ's Hospital: a Retrospect* (prose).
1924		Goes to Japan, as Professor of English Literature at the Imperial University of Tokyo.
	March	His edition of Christopher Smart's *A Song to David*.
1925	June	*Masks of Time*.
	September	Edition of *Shelley and Keats: As they struck their Contemporaries*.
1926	January	*English Poems*.
1927	March	*On the Poems of Henry Vaughan*; an essay and translations of the principal Latin poems.
1928		Returns to England, works on *The Nation*.
	May	*Retreat*.
	July	*Leigh Hunt's* Examiner *Examined*; an account of the newspaper, with extracts and a commentary.
	September	*Japanese Garland*.
		His edition of *The Autobiography of Leigh Hunt* issued.
	November	*Undertones of War* published, with three reprintings in December alone. There was a revised edition in November 1930; a new preface in the World's Classics edition, 1956; a new introduction in the Collins edition, 1964.
1929	June	His edition of *The Poems of William Collins*.
		Nature in English Literature issued by the Hogarth Press.
	September	*Near and Far*.
1930	May	His biography *Leigh Hunt*
	November	*De Bello Germanico*: A fragment of trench history written in 1918.
	December	Publication of *The Poems* 1914-1930.
1931	February	Marriage dissolved.
	March	His editions of *Sketches in the Life of John Clare* and *The Poems of Wilfrid Owen*.
		Becomes Fellow and Tutor in English, Merton College, Oxford.
	November	*Votive Tablets: Studies Chiefly Appreciative of English Authors and Books*.

1932	March	*The Face of England* (prose).
	November	*A Halfway House*.
		Gives the Clark Lectures at Cambridge, *Charles Lamb and His Contemporaries* (published in 1933).
1933	January	*We'll Shift Our Ground*, a novel by Blunden and Sylva Norman, whom he marries this year.
1934	April	*The Mind's Eye* (essays).
	November	*Choice or Chance*.
1937	November	*An Elegy and Other Poems*.
1940		Serves with the University O.T.C., giving instruction in map reading.
1941	January	Publication of *Poems 1930-1940*.
	September	*English Villages* (prose).
1942	February	*Thomas Hardy* published in the 'English Men of Letters' series.
		Marriage to Sylva Norman dissolved.
		Resigns from Merton and returns to the *Times Literary Supplement* as staff writer.
1944	April	*Cricket Country* (prose).
	October	*Shells by a Stream*.
1945	May	Marries Claire Margaret Poynting. There are four daughters by this marriage.
1946	April	His biography *Shelley* published.
1947		Returns to Japan as Cultural Liaison Officer with the British Mission.
1949		Resumes position with the *TLS*.
	October	*After the Bombing*.
1950		Elected to the Japan Academy.
	September	*John Keats* published in 'Writers and their Works' series (revised 1954, 1959, 1966).
	October	Publication of *Edmund Blunden: a Selection of His Poetry and Prose*, edited by Kenneth Hopkins.
1951		Created CBE.
1953		Becomes Professor of English at the University of Hong Kong. During his tenure, returns several times to Japan on lecture tours.
1954	September	His edition of *Poems by Ivor Gurney* published.
	November	*Charles Lamb* published in 'Writers and their Works' series (revised 1964).
1956		Visits China.
		Awarded Queen's Gold Medal for Poetry.

1957	June	Publication of *Poems of Many Years*, selected and arranged by Rupert Hart-Davis.
1958	July	*War Poets 1914-1918* published in 'Writers and their Works' series (revised 1964).
1962		Created Companion of Literature.
	September	*A Hong Kong House*.
1964		Leaves Hong Kong, settles in Long Melford, Suffolk.
1966	February	Elected Professor of Poetry at Oxford, in succession to Robert Graves.
	March	*Eleven Poems*.
1968		Resigns Professorship on medical advice.
	July	Publication of *The Midnight Skaters: Poems for young readers*, chosen and introduced by C. Day Lewis.
1974	20 January	Dies at Long Melford.

THE WAGGONER

The old waggon drudges through the miry lane
   By the skulking pond where the pollards frown,
Notched, dumb, surly images of pain;
   On a dulled earth the night droops down.

Wincing to slow and wistful airs
   The leaves on the shrubbed oaks know their hour,
And the unknown wandering spoiler bares
   The thorned black hedge of a mournful shower.

Small bodies fluster in the dead brown wrack
   As the stumbling shaft-horse jingles past,
And the waggoner flicks his whip a crack:
   The odd light flares on shadows vast

Over the lodges and oasts and byres
   Of the darkened farm; the moment hangs wan
As though nature flagged and all desires.
   But in the dim court the ghost is gone

From the hug-secret yew to the penthouse wall,
   And stooping there seems to listen to
The waggoner leading the gray to the stall,
   As centuries past itself would do.   1919

ALMSWOMEN
for Nancy and Robert

At Quincey's moat the squandering village ends,
And there in the almshouse dwell the dearest friends
Of all the village, two old dames that cling
As close as any trueloves in the spring.
Long, long ago they passed threescore-and-ten,
And in this doll's house lived together then;
All things they have in common, being so poor,
And their one fear, Death's shadow at the door.
Each sundown makes them mournful, each sunrise
Brings back the brightness in their failing eyes.

How happy go the rich fair-weather days
When on the roadside folk stare in amaze
At such a honeycomb of fruit and flowers
As mellows round their threshold; what long hours
They gloat upon their steepling hollyhocks,
Bee's balsams, feathery southernwood, and stocks,
Fiery dragon's-mouths, great mallow leaves
For salves, and lemon-plants in bushy sheaves,
Shagged Esau's-hands with five green finger-tips.
Such old sweet names are ever on their lips.
As pleased as little children where these grow
In cobbled pattens and worn gowns they go,
Proud of their wisdom when on gooseberry shoots
They stuck eggshells to fright from coming fruits
The brisk-billed rascals; pausing still to see
Their neighbour owls saunter from tree to tree,
Or in the hushing half-light mouse the lane
Long-winged and lordly.
                                    But when those hours wane,
Indoors they ponder, scared by the harsh storm
Whose pelting saracens on the window swarm,
And listen for the mail to clatter past
And church clock's deep bay withering on the blast;
They feed the fire that flings a freakish light
On pictured kings and queens grotesquely bright,
Platters and pitchers, faded calendars
And graceful hour-glass trim with lavenders.

Many a time they kiss and cry, and pray
That both be summoned in the selfsame day,
And wiseman linnet tinkling in his cage
End too with them the friendship of old age,
And all together leave their treasured room
Some bell-like evening when the may's in bloom.   1920

THE PIKE

From shadows of rich oaks outpeer
The moss-green bastions of the weir,
Where the quick dipper forages

In elver-peopled crevices,
And a small runlet trickling down the sluice
Gossamer music tires not to unloose.

Else round the broad pool's hush
            Nothing stirs.
Unless sometime a straggling heifer crush
Through the thronged spinney where the pheasant whirs;
    Or martins in a flash
Come with wild mirth to dip their magical wings,
While in the shallow some doomed bulrush swings
At whose hid root the diver vole's teeth gnash.

And nigh this toppling reed, still as the dead
    The great pike lies, the murderous patriarch
    Watching the waterpit sheer-shelving dark,
Where through the plash his lithe bright vassals thread.

    The rose-finned roach and bluish bream
    And staring ruffe steal up the stream
    Hard by their glutted tyrant, now
    Still as a sunken bough.

He on the sandbank lies,
    Sunning himself long hours
With stony gorgon eyes:
    Westward the hot sun lowers.

Sudden the gray pike changes, and quivering poises for slaughter;
    Intense terror wakens around him, the shoals scud awry, but there
        chances
    A chub unsuspecting; the prowling fins quicken, in fury he lances;
And the miller that opens the hatch stands amazed at the whirl
        in the water.   1919

A WATERPIECE

    The wild-rose bush lets loll
Her sweet-breathed petals on the pearl-smooth pool,
The bream-pool overshadowed with the cool
Of oaks where myriad mumbling wings patrol.

19

There the live dimness burrs with droning glees
Of hobby-horses with their starting eyes,
And violet humble-bees and dizzy flies,
That from the dewsprings drink the honeyed lees.

Up the slow stream the immemorial bream
(For when had Death dominion over them?)
Through green pavilions of ghost leaf and stem,
A conclave of blue shadows in a dream,
Glide on; idola that forgotten plan,
Incomparably wise, the doom of man.   1919

A COUNTRY GOD

When groping farms are lanterned up
    And stolchy ploughlands hid in grief,
And glimmering byroads catch the drop
    That weeps from sprawling twig and leaf,
And heavy-hearted spins the wind
    Among the tattered flags of Mirth,—
Then who but I flit to and fro,
With shuddering speech, with mope and mow,
    And glass the eyes of earth?

Then haunt I by some moaning brook
    Where lank and snaky brambles swim,
Or where the hill pines swartly look
    I whirry through the dark and hymn
A dull-voiced dirge and threnody,
    An echo of the sad world's drone
That now appals the friendly stars—
O wail for blind brave youth, whose wars
    Turn happiness to stone.

How rang the cavern-shades of old
    To my melodious pipes, and then
My bright-haired bergomask patrolled
    Each lawn and plot for laughter's din:
Never a sower flung broadcast,
    No hedger brished nor scythesman swung,

Nor maiden trod the purpling press,
But I was by to guard and bless
   And for their solace sung.
   *   *   *
But now the sower's hand is writhed
   In livid death, the bright rhythm stolen,
The gold grain flatted and unscythed,
   The boars in the vineyard, gnarled and sullen,
Havocking the grapes; and the pouncing wind
   Spins the spattered leaves of the glen
In a mockery dance, death's hue and cry;
With all my murmurous pipes flung by
   And summer not to come again.   1918

IN FESTUBERT

Now everything that shadowy thought
   Lets peer with bedlam eyes at me
From alleyways and thoroughfares
   Of cynic and ill memory
Lifts a gaunt head, sullenly stares,
   Shuns me as a child has shunned
A hizzing dragonfly that daps
   Above his muddied pond.

Now bitter frosts, muffling the morn
   In old days, crunching the grass anew;
There, where the floods made fields forlorn
   The glinzy ice grows thicker through,
The pollards glower like mummies when
   Thieves pierce the long-locked pyramid,
Inscrutable as those dead men
   With painted mask and balm-cloth hid;

And all the old delight is cursed
   Redoubling present undelight.
Splinter, crystal, splinter and burst;
   And sear no more with second sight.   1916

SICK-BED

Half dead with fever, here in bed I sprawl,
In candlelight watching the odd flies crawl
Across the ceiling's bleak white desolation;—
Can they not yet have heard of gravitation?—
Hung upside down above the precipice
To doze the night out; ignorance is bliss!
Your blood be on your heads, ridiculous flies.

Dizzying with these, I glare and tantalise
At the motley hides of books which moulder here:
'On Choosing a Career,' 'Ten Thousand a Year';
'Ellis on Sheep,' 'Lamb's Tales,' a doleful Gay,
A has-been Young, dead 'Lives,' vermilion Gray,
And a whole corps of 1790 twelves.
My eye goes blurred along these gruesome shelves,
My brain whirs 'Poems of . . . Poems of . . .' like a clock;
And I stare for my life at the square black ebony block
Of darkness in the open window-frame.
Then my thoughts flash in one white searching flame
On my little lost daughter; I gasp and grasp to see
Her shy smile pondering out who I might be,
Her rathe-ripe rounded cheeks, near-violet eyes.
Long may I stare; her stony fate denies
The vision of her, though tired Fancy's sight
Scrawl with pale curves the dead and scornful night.

All the night's full of questing flights and calls
Of owls and bats, white owls from time-struck walls,
Bats with their shrivelled speech and dragonish wings.
Beneath, a strange step crunches the ash path, where
None goes so late, I know: the mute vast air
Wakes to a great sigh.
                           Now the murmurings,
Cricks, rustlings, knocks, all forms of tiny sound
That have long been happening in my room half-heard,
Grow fast and fierce, each one a ghostly word.
I feel the grutching pixies hedge me round;
'Folly,' sneers courage (and flies). Stealthily creaks
The threshold, fingers fumble, terror speaks,

And, bursting into sweats, I muffle deep
My face in pillows, praying for merciful sleep.

PERCH-FISHING
for G. W. Palmer

On the far hill the cloud of thunder grew
And sunlight blurred below: but sultry blue
Burned yet on the valley water where it hoards
Behind the miller's elmen floodgate boards,
And there the wasps, that lodge them ill-concealed
In the vole's empty house, still drove afield
To plunder touchwood from old crippled trees
And build their young ones their hutched nurseries;
Still creaked the grasshoppers' rasping unison
Nor had the whisper through the tansies run
Nor weather-wisest bird gone home.

                                                How then
Should wry eels in the pebbled shallows ken
Lightning coming? troubled up they stole
To the deep-shadowed sullen water-hole,
Among whose warty snags the quaint perch lair.
As cunning stole the boy to angle there,
Muffling least tread, with no noise balancing through
The hangdog alder-boughs his bright bamboo.
Down plumbed the shuttled ledger, and the quill
On the quicksilver water lay dead still.

A sharp snatch, swirling to-fro of the line,
He's lost, he's won, with splash and scuffling shine
Past the low-lapping brandy-flowers drawn in,
The ogling hunchback perch with needled fin.
And there beside him one as large as he,
Following his hooked mate, careless who shall see
Or what befall him, close and closer yet—
The startled boy might take him in his net
That folds the other.

                              Slow, while on the clay
The other flounces, slow he sinks away.

What agony usurps that watery brain
For comradeship of twenty summers slain,

23

For such delights below the flashing weir
And up the sluice-cut, playing buccaneer
Among the minnows; lolling in hot sun
When bathing vagabonds had drest and done;
Rootling in salty flannel-weed for meal
And river-shrimps, when hushed the trundling wheel;
Snapping the dapping moth, and with new wonder
Prowling through old drowned barges falling asunder.
And O a thousand things the whole year through
They did together, never more to do.   1919

MALEFACTORS

Nailed to these green laths long ago,
You cramp and shrivel into dross,
Blotched with mildews, gnawed with moss,
And now the eye can scarcely know
The snake among you from the kite—
    So sharp does Death's fang bite.

I guess your stories; you were shot
Hovering above the miller's chicks;
And you, coiled on his threshold bricks—
Hissing, you died; and you, Sir Stoat,
Dazzled with stableman's lantern stood
    And tasted crabtree wood.

Here then, you leered-at luckless churls,
Clutched to your clumsy gibbet, shrink
To shapeless orts; hard by the brink
Of this black scowling pond that swirls
To turn the wheel beneath the mill,
    The wheel so long since still.

There's your revenge, the wheel at tether,
The miller gone, the white planks rotten,
The very name of the mill forgotten,
Dimness and silence met together . . . .
Felons of fur and feather, can
    There lurk some crime in man—

In man, your executioner,
Whom here Fate's cudgel battered down?
Did he too filch from squire and clown? . . .
The damp gust makes the ivy whir
Like passing death, the sluices well,
   Dreary as a passing-bell.

                                               1919

CLARE'S GHOST

Pitch-dark night shuts in, and the rising gale
   Is full of the presage of rain,
   And there comes a withered wail
   From the wainscot and jarring pane,
   And a long funeral surge
   Like a wood god's dirge,
Like the wash of the shoreward tides, from the firs on the crest.

The shaking hedges blacken, the last gold flag
   Lowers from the west;
The Advent bell moans wild like a witch hag
   In the storm's unrest,
And the lychgate lantern's candle weaves a shroud,
   And the unlatched gate shrieks loud.

Up fly the smithy sparks, but are baffled from soaring
   By the pelting scurry, and ever
As puff the bellows, a multitude more outpouring
   Die foiled in the endeavour;
And a stranger stands with me here in the glow
Chinked through the door, and marks
      The sparks
Perish in whirlpool wind, and if I go
To the delta of cypress, where the glebe gate cries,
I see him there, with his streaming hair
      And his eyes
Piercing beyond our human firmament,
Lit with a burning deathless discontent.

                                               1917

from **THE SHEPHERD AND OTHER POEMS OF PEACE AND WAR**
(1922)

FOREFATHERS

Here they went with smock and crook,
    Toiled in the sun, lolled in the shade,
Here they mudded out the brook
    And here they hatchet cleared the glade:
Harvest-supper woke their wit,
Huntsman's moon their wooings lit.

From this church they led their brides,
    From this church themselves were led
Shoulder-high; on these waysides
    Sat to take their beer and bread.
Names are gone—what men they were
These their cottages declare.

Names are vanished, save the few
    In the old brown Bible scrawled;
These were men of pith and thew,
    Whom the city never called;
Scarce could read or hold a quill,
Built the barn, the forge, the mill.

On the green they watched their sons
    Playing till too dark to see,
As their fathers watched them once,
    As my father once watched me;
While the bat and beetle flew
On the warm air webbed with dew.

Unrecorded, unrenowned,
    Men from whom my ways begin,
Here I know you by your ground
    But I know you not within—
All is mist, and there survives
Not a moment of your lives.

Like the bee that now is blown
    Honey-heavy on my hand,

From the toppling tansy-throne
   In the green tempestuous land,—
I'm in clover now, nor know
Who made honey long ago.

SPRING NIGHT

Through the smothered air the wicker finds
A muttering voice, 'crick' cries the embered ash,
Sharp rains knap at the panes beyond the blinds,
The flues and eaves moan, the jarred windows clash;
And like a sea breaking its barriers, flooding
New green abysses with untold uproar,
The cataract nightwind whelms the time of budding,
Swooping in sightless fury off the moor
Into our valley. Not a star shines. Who
Would guess the martin and the cuckoo come,
The pear in bloom, the bloom gone from the plum,
The cowslips countless as a morning dew?
So mad it blows, so truceless and so grim,
As if day's host of flowers were a moment's whim.   1920/21

SHEET LIGHTNING

When on the green the rag-tag game had stopt
And red the lights through alehouse curtains glowed,
The clambering brake drove out and took the road.
Then on the stern moors all the babble dropt
Among those merry men, who felt the dew
Sweet to the soul and saw the southern blue
Thronged with heat lightning miles and miles abroad,
Working and whickering, snakish, winged and clawed,
Or like old carp lazily rising and shouldering
Long the slate cloud flank shook with the death-white smouldering:
Yet not a voice.
            The night drooped oven-hot;
Then where the turnpike pierced the black wood plot,
Tongues wagged again and each man felt the grim
Destiny of the hour speaking through him,

And then tales came of dwarfs on Starling Hill
And those young swimmers drowned at the roller Mill,
Where on the drowsiest noon the undertow
Famishing for life boiled like a pot below:
And how two higglers at the Walnut Tree
Had curst the Lord in thunderstorm and He
Had struck them dead as soot with lightning then—
It left the tankards whole, it chose the men.
Many a lad and many a lass was named
Who once stept bold and proud; but death had tamed
Their revel on the eve of May; cut short
The primrosing and promise of good sport,
Shut up the score book, laid the ribbands by.

Such bodings mustered from the fevered sky;
But now the spring well through the honeycomb
Of scored stone rumbling tokened them near home,
The whip lash clacked, the jog-trot sharpened, all
Sang Farmer's Boy as loud as they could bawl,
And at the Walnut Tree the homeward brake
Stopt for hoarse ribaldry to brag and slake.

The weary wildfire faded from the dark;
While this one damned the parson, that the clerk;
And anger's balefire forked from the unbared blade
At word of things gone wrong or stakes not paid:

While Joe the driver stooped with oath to find
A young jack rabbit in the roadway, blind
Or dazzled by the lamps, as stiff as steel
With fear. Joe beat its brain out on the wheel.

CLOUDY JUNE

Above the hedge the spearman thistle towers
And thinks himself the god of all he sees;
But nettles jostle fearless where he glowers,
Like old and stained and sullen tapestries;
And elbowing hemlocks almost turn to trees,
Proud as the sweetbriar with her bubble flowers,

28

    Where puft green spider cowers
    To trap the toiling bees.

Here joy shall muse what melancholy tells,
And melancholy smile because of joy,
Whether the poppy breathe arabian spells
To make them friends, or whistling gipsy-boy
Sound them a truce that nothing comes to cloy.
No sunray burns through this slow cloud, nor swells
    Noise save the browsing-bells,
    Half sorrow and half joy.

Night comes; from fens where blind grey castles frown
A veiled moon ventures on the cavernous sky.
No stir, no tassel-tremble on the down:
Mood dims to nothing: atom-like I lie
Where nightjars burr and yapping fox steps by
And hedgehogs wheeze and play in glimmering brown;
    And my swooned passions drown,
    Nor tell me I am I.

MOLE CATCHER

With coat like any mole's, as soft and black,
And hazel bows bundled beneath his arm,
And long-helved spade and rush bag on his back
The trapper plods alone about the farm
And spies new mounds in the ripe pasture-land,
And where the lob-worms writhe up in alarm
And easy sinks the spade, he takes his stand
Knowing the moles' dark highroad runs below:
Then sharp and square he chops the turf, and day
Gloats on the opened turnpike through the clay.

Out from his wallet hurry pin and prong,
And trap, and noose to tie it to the bow;
And then his grand arcanum, oily and strong,
Found out by his forefather years ago
To scent the peg and witch the moles along.
The bow is earthed and arched ready to shoot

And snatch the death-knot fast round the first mole
Who comes and snuffs well pleased and tries to root
Past the sly nose peg; back again is put
The mould, and death left smirking in the hole.
The old man goes and tallies all his snares
And finds the prisoners there and takes his toll.

And moles to him are only moles; but hares
See him afield and scarcely cease to nip
Their dinners, for he harms not them; he spares
The drowning fly that of his ale would sip
And throws the ant the crumbs of comradeship.
And every time he comes into his yard
Grey linnet knows he brings the groundsel sheaf
And clatters round the cage to be unbarred
And on his finger whistles twice as hard.—
What his old vicar says, is his belief.
In the side pew he sits and hears the truth
And never misses once to ring his bell
On Sundays night and morn, nor once since youth
Has heard the chimes afield, but has heard tell
There's not a peal in England sounds so well.

THE SCYTHE STRUCK BY LIGHTNING

A thick hot haze had choked the valley grounds
Long since, the dogday sun had gone his rounds
Like a dull coal half lit with sulky heat;
And leas were iron, ponds were clay, fierce beat
The blackening flies round moody cattle's eyes.
Wasps on the mudbanks seemed a hornet's size
That on the dead roach battened. The plough's increase
Stood under a curse.
                         Behold, the far release!
Old wisdom breathless at her cottage door
'Sounds of abundance' mused, and heard the roar
Of marshalled armies in the silent air,
And thought Elisha stood beside her there,
And clacking reckoned ere the next nightfall
She'd turn the looking-glasses to the wall.

Faster than armies out of the burnt void
The hourglass clouds innumerably deployed,
And when the hay-folks next looked up, the sky
Sags black above them; scarce is time to fly.
And most run for their cottages; but Ward,
The mower for the inn beside the ford,
And slow strides he with shouldered scythe still bare,
While to the covert leaps the great-eyed hare.

As he came in the dust snatched up and whirled
Hung high, and like a bell-rope whipped and twirled;
The brazen light glared round, the haze resolved
Into demoniac shapes bulged and convolved.
Well might poor ewes afar make bleatings wild,
Though this old trusting mower sat and smiled,
For from the hush of many days the land
Had waked itself: and now on every hand
Shrill swift alarm-notes, cries and counter-cries,
Lowings and crowings came and throbbing sighs.
Now atom lightning brandished on the moor,
Then out of sullen drumming came the roar
Of thunder joining battle east and west:
In hedge and orchard small birds durst not rest,
Flittering like dead leaves and like wisps of straws,
And the cuckoo called again, for without pause
Oncoming voices in the vortex burred.
The storm came toppling like a wave, and blurred
In grey the trees that like black steeples towered.
The sun's last yellow died. Then who but cowered?
Down ruddying darkness floods the hideous flash,
And pole to pole the cataract whirlwinds clash.

Alone within the tavern parlour still
Sat the grey mower, pondering his God's will,
And flinching not to flame or bolt, that swooped
With a great hissing rain till terror drooped
In weariness: and then there came a roar
Ten-thousand-fold, he saw not, was no more—
But life bursts on him once again, and blood
Beats droning round, and light comes in a flood.

He stares and sees the sashes battered awry,
The wainscot shivered, the crocks shattered, and nigh,
His twisted scythe, melted by its fierce foe,
Whose Parthian shot struck down the chimney. Slow
Old Ward lays hand to his old working-friend,
And thanking God Whose mercy did defend
His servant, yet must drop a tear or two
And think of times when that old scythe was new,
And stands in silent grief, nor hears the voices
Of many a bird that through the land rejoices,
Nor sees through the smashed panes the seagreen sky,
That ripens into blue, nor knows the storm is by.

THE POOR MAN'S PIG

Ready fallen plum-bloom stars the green
        And apple-boughs as knarred as old toads' backs
Wear their small roses ere a rose is seen;
        The building thrush watches old Job who stacks
The bright-peeled osiers on the sunny fence,
        The pent sow grunts to hear him stumping by,
And tries to push the bolt and scamper thence,
        But her ringed snout still keeps her to the sty. *6 lines missing*

Then out he lets her run; away she snorts
In bundling gallop for the cottage door.

FESTUBERT, 1916

Tired with dull grief, grown old before my day,
I sit in solitude and only hear
Long silent laughters, murmurings of dismay,
The lost intensities of hope and fear;
In those old marshes yet the rifles lie,
On the thin breastwork flutter the grey rags,
The very books I read are there—and I
Dead as the men I loved, wait while life drags

Its wounded length from those sad streets of war
Into green places here, that were my own;
But now what once was mine is mine no more,
I look for such friends here and I find none.

32

With hungry hubbub begging crusts and orts.
Then like the whirlwind bumping round once more
Nuzzling the dog, making the pullets run,
And sulky as a child when her play's done.

With such strong gentleness and tireless will
Those ruined houses seared themselves in me,
Passionate I look for their dumb story still,
And the charred stub outspeaks the living tree.

I rise up at the singing of a bird
And scarcely knowing slink along the lane,
I dare not give a soul a look or word
For all have homes and none's at home in vain:
Deep red the rose burned in the grim redoubt,
The self-sown wheat around was like a flood,
In the hot path the lizard lolled time out,
The saints in broken shrines were bright as blood.

Sweet Mary's shrine between the sycamores!
There we would go, my friend of friends and I,
And snatch long moments from the grudging wars;
Whose dark made light intense to see them by . . .
Shrewd bit the morning fog, the whining shots
Spun from the wrangling wire; then in warm swoon
The sun hushed all but the cool orchard plots,
We crept in the tall grass and slept till noon.

THIRD YPRES
A Reminiscence

Triumph! how strange, how strong had triumph come
On weary hate of foul and endless war,
When from its grey gravecloths awoke anew
The summer day. Among the tumbled wreck
Of fascined lines and mounds the light was peering,
Half-smiling upon us, and our new-found pride;—
The terror of the waiting night outlived;
The time too crowded for the heart to count
All the sharp cost of friends killed on the assault.
No sap of all the octopus had held us,
Here stood we trampling down the ancient tyrant.
So shouting dug we among the monstrous pits.

Amazing quiet fell upon the waste,
Quiet intolerable, to those who felt

The hurrying batteries beyond the masking hills
For their new parley setting themselves in array
In crafty fourms unmapped.
                                No, these, smiled faith,
Are dumb for the reason of their overthrow.
They move not back, they lie among the crews
Twisted and choked, they'll never speak again.
Only the copse where once might stand a shrine
Still clacked and suddenly hissed its bullets by.

The War would end, the Line was on the move,
And at a bound the impassable was passed.
We lay and waited with extravagant joy.

Now dulls the day and chills; comes there no word
From those who swept through our new lines to flood
The lines beyond? but little comes, and so
Sure as a runner time himself's accosted.
And the slow moments shake their heavy heads,
And croak, 'They're done, they'll none of them get through.'
They're done, they've all died on the entanglements,
The wire stood up like an unplashed hedge, and thorned
With giant spikes—and there they've paid the bill.

Then comes the black assurance, then the sky's
Mute misery lapses into trickling rain,
That wreathes and swims and soon shuts in our world.
And those distorted guns, that lay past use,
Why—miracles not over!—all a firing,
The rain's no cloak from their sharp eyes. And you,
Poor signaller, you I passed by this emplacement,
You whom I warned, poor dare-devil, waving your flags,
Among this screeching I pass you again and shudder
At the lean green flies upon the red flesh madding.
Runner, stand by a second. Your message.—He's gone,
Falls on a knee, and his right hand uplifted
Claws his last message from his ghostly enemy,
Turns stone-like. Well I like him, that young runner,
But there's no time for that. O now for the word
To order us flash from these drowning roaring traps
And even hurl upon that snarling wire?
Why are our guns so impotent?

             The grey rain,
Steady as the sand in an hourglass on this day,
Where through the window the red lilac looks
And all's so still, the chair's odd click is noise,—
The rain is all heaven's answer, and with hearts
Past reckoning we are carried into night,
And even sleep is nodding here and there.

The second night steals through the shrouding rain,
We in our numb thought crouching long have lost
The mockery triumph, and in every runner
Have urged the mind's eye see the triumph to come,
The sweet relief, the straggling out of hell
Into whatever burrows may be given
For life's recall. Then the fierce destiny speaks.
This was the calm, we shall look back for this.
The hour is come; come, move to the relief!
Dizzy we pass the mule-strewn track where once
The ploughman whistled as he loosed his team;
And where he turned home—hungry on the road
The leaning pollard marks us hungrier turning.
We crawl to save the remnant who have torn
Back from the tentacled wire, those whom no shell
Has charred into black carcasses—Relief!
They grate their teeth until we take their room,
And through the churn of moonless night and mud
And flaming burst and sour gas we are huddled
Into the ditches where they bawl sense awake
And in a frenzy that none could reason calm
(Whimpering some, and calling on the dead)
They turn away; as in a dream they find
Strength in their feet to bear back that strange whim
Their body.

         At the noon of the dreadful day
Our trench and death's is on a sudden stormed
With huge and shattering salvoes, the clay dances
In founts of clods around the concrete sties
Where still the brain devises some last armour
To live out the poor limbs.

This wrath's oncoming

Found four of us together in a pillbox,
Skirting the abyss of madness with light phrases,
White and blinking, in false smiles grimacing.
The demon grins to see the game, a moment
Passes, and—still the drum-tap dongs my brain
To a whirring void—through the great breach above me
The light comes in with icy shock and the rain
Horridly drips. Doctor, talk, talk! if dead
Or stunned I know not; the stinking powdered concrete,
The lyddite turns me sick—my hair's all full
Of this smashed concrete. O I'll drag you, friends,
Out of the sepulchre into the light of day:
For this is day, the pure and sacred day.
And while I squeak and gibber over you,
Out of the wreck a score of field-mice nimble,
And tame and curious look about them. (These
Calmed me, on these depended my salvation.)

There comes my serjeant, and by all the powers
The wire is holding to the right battalion
And I can speak—but I myself first spoken
Hear a known voice now measured even to madness
Call me by name: 'for God's sake send and help us,
Here in a gunpit, all headquarters done for,
Forty or more, the nine-inch came right through.
All splashed with arms and legs, and I myself
The only one not killed, not even wounded.
You'll send—God bless you.' The more monstrous fate
Shadows our own, the mind droops doubly burdened,
Nay all for miles our anguish groans and bleeds,
A whole sweet countryside amuck with murder,
Each moment puffed into a year with death.

Still wept the rain, roared guns,
Still swooped into the swamps of flesh and blood
All to the drabness of uncreation sunk,
And all thought dwindled to a moan,—Relieve!
But who with what command can now relieve
The dead men from that chaos, or my soul?

DEATH OF CHILDHOOD BELIEFS

There the puddled lonely lane,
 Lost among the red swamp sallows,
Gleams through drifts of summer rain
 Down to ford the sandy shallows,
Where the dewberry brambles crane.

And the stream in cloven clay
 Round the bridging sheep-gate stutters,
Wind-spun leaves burn silver-grey,
 Far and wide the blue moth flutters
Over swathes of warm new hay.

Scrambling boys with mad to-do
 Paddle in the sedges' hem,
Ever finding joy anew;
 Clocks toll time out—not for them,
With what years to frolic through!

How shall I return and how
 Look once more on those old places!
For Time's cloud is on me now
 That each day, each hour effaces
Visions once on every bough.

Stones could talk together then,
 Jewels lay for hoes to find,
Each oak hid King Charles agen,
 Ay, nations in his powdered rind;
Sorcery lived with homeless men.

Spider Dick, with cat's green eyes
 That could pierce stone walls, has flitted—
By some hedge he shakes and cries,
 A lost man, half-starved, half-witted,
Whom the very stoats despise.

Trees on hill-tops then were Palms,
 Closing pilgrims' arbours in;
David walked there singing Psalms;
 Out of the clouds white seraphin
Leaned to watch us fill our bin.

Where's the woodman now to tell
    Will o' the Whisp's odd fiery anger?
Where's the ghost to toll the bell
    Startling midnight with its clangour
Till the wind seemed but a knell?

Drummers jumping from the tombs
    Banged and thumped all through the town,
Past shut shops and silent rooms
    While the flaming spires fell down;—
Now but dreary thunder booms.

Smuggler trapped in headlong spate,
    Smuggler's mare with choking whinney,
Well I knew your fame, your fate;
    By the ford and shaking spinney
Where you perished I would wait,

Half in glory, half in fear,
    While the fierce flood, trough and crest,
Whirled away the shepherd's gear,
    And sunset wildfire coursed the west,
Crying Armageddon near.

THE CANAL

    Where so dark and still
Slept the water, never changing,
From the glad sport in the meadows
    Oft I turned me.

    Fear would strike me chill
On the clearest day in summer,
Yet I loved to stand and ponder
    Hours together

    By the tarred bridge rail—
There the lockman's vine-clad window,
Mirrored in the tomb-like water,
    Stared in silence

        Till, deformed and pale
In the sunken cavern shadows,
One by one imagined demons
        Scowled upon me.

        Barges passed me by,
With their unknown surly masters
And small cabins, whereon some rude
        Hand had painted

        Trees and castles high.
Cheerly stepped the towing horses,
And the women sung their children
        Into slumber.

        Barges, too, I saw
Drowned in mud, drowned, drowned long ages,
Their grey ribs but seen in summer,
        Their names never:

        In whose silted maw
Swarmed great eels, the priests of darkness,
Old as they, who came at midnight
        To destroy me.

        Like one blind and lame
Who by some new sense has vision
And strikes deadlier than the strongest
        Went this water.

        Many an angler came,
Went his ways; and I would know them,
Some would smile and give me greeting,
        Some kept silence—

        Most, one old dragoon
Who had never a morning hallo,
But with stony eye strode onward
        Till the water,

        On a silent noon,
That had watched him long, commanded:

Whom he answered, leaping headlong
    To self-murder.

    'Fear and fly the spell,'
Thus my Spirit sang beside me;
Then once more I ranged the meadows,
    Yet still brooded,

    When the threefold knell
Sounded through the haze of harvest—
Who had found the lame blind water
    Swift and seeing?

from **TO NATURE** *(1923)*

RURAL ECONOMY (1917)

There was winter in those woods,
    And still it was July:
There were Thule solitudes
    With thousands huddling nigh;
There the fox had left his den,
The scraped holes hid not stoats but men.

To these woods the rumour teemed
    Of peace five miles away;
In sight, hills hovered, houses gleamed
    Where last perhaps we lay
Till the cockerels bawled bright morning and
The hours of life slipped the slack hand.

In sight, life's farms sent forth their gear,
    Here rakes and ploughs lay still,
Yet, save some curious clods, all here
    Was raked and ploughed with a will.
The sower was the ploughman too,
And iron seeds broadcast he threw.

What husbandry could outdo this?
    With flesh and blood he fed
The planted iron that nought amiss
    Grew thick and swift and red,
And in a night though ne'er so cold
Those acres bristled a hundredfold.

Nay, even the wood as well as field
    This ruseful farmer knew
Could be reduced to plough and tilled,
    And if he planned, he'd do;
The field and wood, all bone-fed loam,
Shot up a roaring harvest-home.

WATER MOMENT

The silver eel slips through the waving weeds,
And in the tunnelled shining stone recedes;
The earnest eye surveys the crystal pond
And guards the cave: the sweet shoals pass beyond.
The watery jewels that these have for eyes,
The tiger streaks of him that hindmost plies,
The red-gold wings that smooth their daring paces,
The sunlight dancing about their airs and graces,
Burn that strange watcher's heart; then the sly brain
Speaks, all the dumb shoal shrieks, and by the stone
The silver death writhes with the chosen one.

THE STILL HOUR

As in the silent darkening room I lay,
While winter's early evening, heavy-paced
As ploughman from our swarthy soil, groped on
From the cold mill upon the horizon hill
And over paddocks to the neighbouring lodges
And lay as I, tired out with colourless toil,
Inert, the lubber fiend, whose puffing drowse
The moon's dawn scarce would fret, through the low cloud,—
When thus at ebb I lay, my silence flowered

Gently as later bloom into a warm
Harmonious chiming; like a listener I
Was hushed. The spirits of remembrance all
In one concent made music, a flood, a haze,
A vista all to one ripe blushing blended.

That summer veil of sweet sound then awhile
Gave me clear voices, as though from rosy distance
Whence drifting multitude of song had come,
The several bells each in his round were heard;
The tower that throned them seen, and even the golden
Chanticleer that frolicked on its top.
From my broad murmuring ode there came fair forth
The cries of playing children on one day,
At one blue dewy hour, by one loved green;
And then the brook was tumbling lit like gems
Down its old sluice, and old boy-heroes stood
To catch its sparkling stonefish—I heard even
The cry that hailed the chestnut tench's downfall
In the next swim, that strange historic victim.
From church and pasture, sweetheart and sworn friend,
From the hill's hopgrounds to the lowest leas
In the rook-routed vale, from the blind boy
Who lived by me to the dwellers in the heath,
From robins building in the gipsy's kettle
Thrown in our hedge, to waterfowl above
The mouldering mill, distinct and happy now
Ten thousand singings from my childhood rang.

And time seemed stealing forward as they sounded,
The syllables of first delights passed; years
That ended childhood with their secret sigh
Uttered their joys, still longed-for, still enshrined.
And then what voices?
                              Straight, it seemed, from those,
While a long age was silent as the grave,
The utterance passed to that stern course of chances
That crowded far-off Flanders with ourselves.
I heard the signallers lead the strong battalion
With bold songs flying to the breeze like banners,
The quiet courage once again of Daniells

By some few words built up a fort around me,
And while the long guns clattered through the towns
I, rather, heard the clack of market-women,
The hostel's gramophone and gay girls fooling,
And chants in painted churches, and my friend's
Lively review of Flemish contraries.
Or, was not this the green Bethune canal
And these our shouts, our laughs, our awkward plunges,
While summer's day went cloudless to its close?
There shone the Ancre, red-leafed woods above it,
The blue speed of its waters swirled through causeways;
There from his hammock in the apple orchard
Up sprang old Swain and rallied intruding youngsters.
The company now fell in, to the very yard,
And once again marched eager towards the Somme,
And there, a score of voices leapt again
After a hare that left her seat in the corn.
I think I'd know that twinkling field to-day.

So in a swift succession my still hour
Heard Flanders voices, in the line direct
From those of childhood; but at last the host
In such confusion as nigh stopt my breath
With glory and anguish striving, drew far on
And all became a drone, that in decline
From summer's bravery changed to autumn chill.
And as the music vague and piteous grew,
I saw the mist die from its pleasant charm,
Now fierce with early frost its numb shroud lay
Along sad ridges, and as one aloof
I saw the praying rockets mile on mile
Climb all too weak from those entangled there,
Climb for the help that would not help them there;
And even these purple vapours died away
And left the surly evening brown as clay
Upon those ridges battered into chaos
Whence one deep moaning, one deep moaning came.

HARVEST

So there's my year, the twelvemonth duly told,
Since last I climbed this brow and gloated round
Upon the lands heaped with their wheaten gold,
And now again they spread with wealth imbrowned,
    And thriftless I meanwhile,
What honeycombs have I to take, what sheaves to pile?

I see some shrivelled fruits upon my tree,
And gladly would self-kindness feign them sweet;
The bloom smelled heavenly, can these stragglers be
The sum of that bright birth? and this wry wheat,
    Can this be from those spires
Which I, or fancy, saw leap to the spring sun's fires?

I peer, and count, but anxious is not rich,
My harvest is not come, the weeds run high,
Even poison-berries ramping from the ditch
Have stormed the undefended ridges by;
    What Michaelmas is mine!
The fields I thought to serve, for sturdier tillage pine.

But, hush—Earth's valleys sweet in leisure lie,
And I among them, wandering up and down,
Will taste their berries, like a bird or fly,
And of their gleanings make both feast and crown;
    The Sun's eye laughing looks,
And Earth accuses none that goes among her stooks.

ERAS

The trunks of trees which I knew glorious green,
Which I saw felled last year, already show
Rust-red their rounds, the twisting path between
Their hulks takes its new way trod plain as though
It went this way since years and years ago.
The plough I saw my friend so often guide,

Snapped on the sly snag at the spinney side,
Lies rusting there where brambles overflow;
As gulfed in limbo lake as buried coins,
Which once both bread and wine, now nothing mean.
The spider dates it not but spins in the heat,
For what's time past? but present time is sweet.
Aye, in that churchyard lies fruit of our loins,
—The child who bright as pearl shone into breath
With the Egyptian's first-born shares coeval death.

A DREAM

Unriddle this.   Last night my dream
Took me along a sullen stream,
A water drifting black and ill,
With idiot swirls, and silent still.
As if it had been Pactolus
And I of gold sands amorous
I went determined on its bank,
Stopped in the breath of dim and dank,
And in my hand (in dream's way) took
A living fish to bait my hook,
A living fish, not gudgeon quite
Nor dace nor roach, a composite;
Then ghoulishly with fingers, yet
With aching mind, I strove to get
The pang of shackling metal through
The mouth of that poor mad perdu,
And, (ran the bitter fancy's plot),
To tie his body in a knot.
While thus I groped and grasped and coiled
And he in horror flapped and foiled,
I saw how on the clay around
Young shining fishes leapt and clowned,
And often turned their eyes on me,
Begging their watery liberty,
Most sad and odd. But, thought I, now
I have no time for helping you,
And then at length my bait was hooked,
His shuddering tail grotesquely crooked.

Black was the secret-dimpling stream,
I flounced him to the line's extreme,
And then, his mercy! gladdening me
Who just had been his agony,
Some monstrous mouth beat out his brain,
The line cut wide its graphs of strain.
I knew my prize, and fought my best,
With thought and thew—then the fight ceased.
Sobbing I feared the quarry gone,
But no, the dead-weight showed him on.
Slow to the mould I pulled the huge
Half-legend from his subterfuge,
And as he from the water thrust
His head, and cleared its scurf and must,
Two eyes as old as Adam stared
On mine. And now he lay unbared:
My glory! On the bleak bank lay
A carcass effigy in clay,
A trunk of vague and lifeless mass
Such as might lie beneath filmed glass,
Where on the pane the buzzing fly
Batters to win the desperate sky.

INTIMATIONS OF MORTALITY

I am only the phrase
Of an unknown musician;
By a gentle voice spoken
I stole forth and met you
In halcyon days.
Yet, frail as I am, you yourself shall be broken
Before we are parted; I have but one mission,—
Till death to beset you.

I am only the glowing
Of a dead afternoon,
When you, full of wonder,
Your hand in your mother's,
Up great streets were going.
Pale was my flame, and the cold sun fell under

The blue heights of houses; but I shall gleam on
  In your life past all others.

   I am only the bloom
  Of an apple-tree's roses,
  That stooped to the grass
  Where the robins were nesting
  In an old vessel's womb.
Dead is the tree, and your steps may not pass
The place where it smiled; but I'll come, till death closes
  My ghostly molesting.

  —You phantoms, pursue me,
  Be upon me, amaze me,
  Though nigh all your presence
  With sorrow enchant me;
  With sorrow renew me!
Songless and gleamless I near no new pleasance,
In subtle returnings of ecstasy raise me,
  To my winding-sheet haunt me!

STRANGE PERSPECTIVE

Happy the herd is that in the heat of summer
Wades in the waters where the willows cool them,
From murmuring midday that singes the meadow;
And turns very tansies, fire-flowers, tindery.
Naked at noon there, naughtiness too wantons,
From bank bold jumping, and bough down dandling,
Of chimed hour chainless, and churlish duty.
I see the glad set, who am far off sentenced;
Their lily limbs dazzle over long dry pastures,
And rude though ridges are risen between us,
Miles of mountains morosely upthrusting;
And dim and downward my gaze now droops,
My pool beyond pasture by a strange perspective
Is plain, and plunging its playmates gleam,
Hustling the staid herd into hazardous shadows.

TWO VOICES

'There's something in the air,' he said,
   In the large parlour cool and bare,
The plain words in his hearers bred
   A tumult, yet in silence there
All waited; wryly gay, he left the phrase,
Ordered the march and bade us go our ways.

'We're going South, man'; as he spoke
   The howitzer with huge ping-bang
Racked the light hut; as thus he broke
   The death-news, bright the skylarks sang;
He took his riding-crop and humming went
Among the apple-trees all bloom and scent.

Now far withdraws the roaring night
   Which wrecked our flower after the first
Of those two voices; misty light
   Shrouds Thiepval Wood and all its worst:
But still 'There's something in the air' I hear,
And still 'We're going South, man' deadly near.

PREPARATIONS FOR VICTORY

My soul, dread not the pestilence that hags
The valley; flinch not you, my body young,
At these great shouting smokes and snarling jags
Of fiery iron: the dice may not be flung
As yet that claims you. Manly move among
These ruins, and what you must do, do well;
Look, here are gardens, there mossed boughs are hung
With apples whose bright cheeks none might excel,
And here's a house as yet unshattered by a shell.

'I'll do my best,' the soul makes sad reply,
'And I will mark the yet unmurdered tree,
The relics of dear homes that court the eye,
And yet I see them not as I would see.
Hovering between, a ghostly enemy

Sickens the light, and poisoned, withered, wan,
The least defiled turns desperate to me.'
The body, poor unpitied Caliban,
Parches and sweats and grunts to win the name of Man.

Hours, days, eternities, like swelling waves
Pass on, and still we drudge in this dark maze,
The bombs and coils and cans by strings of slaves
Are borne to serve the coming day of days;
Pale sleep in slimy cellars scarce allays
With its brief blank the burden. Look, we lose;
The sky is gone, the lightless drenching haze
Of rainstorm chills the bone; earth, air are foes,
The black fiend leaps brick-red as life's last picture goes.

ZERO

O rosy red, O torrent splendour
Staining all the Orient sky,
O celestial work of wonder,
A million mornings in one dye!

What, does the artist of creation
Try some new plethora of flame,
For his eyes' fresh fascination,
Has the old cosmic fire grown tame?

In what subnatural strange awaking
Is this body, which seems mine?
These feet towards that blood-burst making,
These ears which thunder, these hands which twine

On grotesque iron? Icy-clear
The air of a mortal day shocks sense,
My shaking men pant after me here.
The acid vapours hovering dense,

The fury whizzing in dozens down,
The clattering rafters, clods calcined,
The blood in the flints and the trackway brown,
I see I am clothed and in my right mind;

The dawn but hangs behind the goal,
What is that artist's joy to me?
Here limps poor Jock with a gash in the poll,
His red blood now is the red I see.

The swooning white of him, and that red!
These bombs in boxes, the craunch of shells,
The second-hand flitting round; ahead!
It's plain, we were born for this, nought else.

THE ANCRE AT HAMEL

Where tongues were loud and hearts were light
  I heard the Ancre flow;
Waking oft at the mid of night
  I heard the Ancre flow.
I heard it crying, that sad rill,
  Below the painful ridge,
By the burnt unraftered mill
  And the relic of a bridge.

And could this sighing water seem
  To call me far away,
And its pale word dismiss as dream
  The voices of to-day?
The voices in the bright room chilled
  And that mourned on alone,
The silence of the full moon filled
  With that brook's troubling tone.

The struggling Ancre had no part
  In these new hours of mine,
And yet its stream ran through my heart,
  I heard it grieve and pine,
As if its rainy tortured blood
  Had swirled into my own,
When by its battered bank I stood
  And shared its wounded moan.

THE DAIMYO'S POND

The swallows come on swift and daring wings,
Their daring wings to dip with pure delight
In the mild pond; once more the kind fate brings
My heart that moment, and the world is bright.
The lilies there, the white ones and the red,
From the green cloudy deeps look up to heaven,
And antique holm-oaks sheltering their calm bed
Seem blessing Earth for such a sweet trust given.

Look, how that old man, face like parchment tanned,
Wrinkled, mouth-shrivelled, silently is come
To the high bank, a bucket in his hand—
He beats upon it as it were a drum:
He beats a solemn summoning monotone,
And through the secrecies that under shroud,
The water-shapes steal towards his gonging drone,
The lonelinesses gather in a crowd.

Moon-pallid some come gliding through the green,
Great fishes, yet for phantoms passing well;
Others like opals rosy-rayed convene,
Jewels of June waters, to that simple bell;
Dark as barbaric dreams, there others swim,
And now to that old labourer's wish a host
Of splendours circle mingling, to the brim
Fanning and fawning, flame and dream and ghost.

Would that I might by means as plain as this
Bring many a mystery from life's shadowy pool,
Enchant the live gems from the unknown abyss,
And make them seen, the strangely beautiful.
What measured syllables must I resound,
Oh, what most simple and most secret spell
For hidden fancies waits there to be found?
Who knows that incantation, and will tell?

WINTER: EAST ANGLIA

In a frosty sunset
    So fiery red with cold
The footballers' onset
    Rings out glad and bold;
Then boys from daily tether
    With famous dogs at heel
In starlight meet together
    And to farther hedges steal;
Where the rats are pattering
    In and out the stacks,
Owls with hatred chattering
    Swoop at the terriers' backs.
And, frost forgot, the chase grows hot
    Till a rat's a foolish prize,
But the cornered weasel stands his ground,
Shrieks at the dogs and boys set round,
Shrieks as he knows they stand all round,
    And hard as winter dies.

THE MIDNIGHT SKATERS

The hop-poles stand in cones,
    The icy pond lurks under,
The pole-tops steeple to the thrones
    Of stars, sound gulfs of wonder;
But not the tallest there, 'tis said,
Could fathom to this pond's black bed.

Then is not death at watch
    Within those secret waters?
What wants he but to catch
    Earth's heedless sons and daughters?
With but a crystal parapet
Between, he has his engines set.

Then on, blood shouts, on, on,
    Twirl, wheel and whip above him,
Dance on this ball-floor thin and wan,
    Use him as though you love him;
Court him, elude him, reel and pass,
And let him hate you through the glass.

THE PUZZLE

The cuckoo with a strong flute,
The orchard with a mild sigh,
Bird and blossom so salute
    The rainbow sky.

The brown herd in the green shade,
The parson in his lawn chair,
Poor and gentry both evade
    The furnace air.

The moon-inveigled mushroom,
The crocus with her frail horn,
Gaze in dumb dread through the gloom
    Of late moist morn.

The dead leaf on the highlands,
The old tramp on the mill drove,
Each whirls on nor understands
    God's freezing love.

WARNING TO TROOPS

What soldier guessed that where the stream descended
In country dance beneath the colonnade
Of elms which cooled the halted troop, it played
Sly music, barely noted, never ended?
Or who, from war's concerns a moment missed,
At some church door turned white as came to him
One gold note struck by hidden organist,
One note long-drawn through caverns cool and dim?

O marcher, hear. But when thy route and tramp
Pause by some falling stream, or church's door,
Be the deaf adder; bear not back to camp
That embryo music. Double not thy war.
Know not that sweet prelusion. March, sing, roar,
Lest a mad silence gnaw thee evermore.

IN A COUNTRY CHURCHYARD

Earth is a quicksand; yon square tower
    Would still seem bold,
But its bleak flinty strength each hour
    Is losing hold.

Small sound of gasping undertow
    In this green bed!
Who shuts the gate will shut it slow,
    Here sleep the dead.

Here sleep, or slept; here, chance they sleep,
    Though still this soil
As mad and clammed as shoals acreep
    Around them boil.

The earth slips down to the low brown
    Moss-eaten wall
Each year, and nettles and grasses drown
    Its crumbling crawl.

The dog-rose and ox-daisies on
    Time's tide come twirling,
And bubble and die where Joy is gone—
    Sleep well, my darling.

Seldom the sexton with shrewd grin
    Near thy grave-cloth,
With withered step and mumble thin
    Awakes eve's moth.

Not a farm boy dares here destroy,
    Through red-toothed nettles,

The chiff-chaff's nest, and strew the shells
    Like fallen petals.

The silver-hooded moth upsprings,
    The silver hour,
And wanders on with happy wings
    By the hush tower,

That reels and whirs, and never drops,
    That still is going;
For quicksand not an instant stops
    Its deadly flowing.

And is Joy up and dancing there
    Where deepening blue
Asks a new star? is that her hair
    There freshed with dew?

Here, O the skull of some small wretch,
    Some slaughtered jot,
Bones white as leaf-strigs or chopped twitch,
    Thus turned fate's plot.

So lies thy skull? This earth, even this
    Like quicksand weaves.
Sleep well, my darling, though I kiss
    Lime or dead leaves.

Sleep in the flux as on the breast,
    In the vortex loll;
In mid simoom, my innocence, rest;
    In lightning's soul

Bower thyself! But, joyous eyes,
    The deeps drag dull—
O morning smile and song, so lies
    Thy tiny skull?

SOLUTIONS

The swallow flew like lightning over the green
And through the gate-bars (a hand's breadth between);
He hurled his blackness at that chink and won;
The problem scarcely rose and it was done.

The spider, chance-confronted with starvation,
Took up another airy situation;
His working legs, as it appeared to me,
Had mastered practical geometry.

The old dog dreaming in his frowsy cask
Enjoyed his rest and did not drop his task;
He knew the person of 'no fixed abode,'
And challenged as he shuffled down the road.

These creatures which (Buffon and I agree)
Lag far behind the human faculty
Worked out the question set with satisfaction
And promptly took the necessary action.

By this successful sang-froid I, employed
On 'Who wrote Shakespeare?' justly felt annoyed,
And seeing an evening primrose by the fence
Beheaded it for blooming insolence.

DEPARTURE

The beech leaves caught in a moment's gust
Run like bowled pennies in the autumn's dust
        And topple; frost like rain
Comes spangling down; through the prismy trees
Phœbus mistakes our horse for his,
        Such glory clothes his mane.

The stream makes his glen music alone
And plays upon shell and pot and stone—

Our life's after-refrain;
Till in the sky the tower's old song
Reads us the hour, and reads it wrong,
And carter-like comes whistling along
Our casual Anglian train.

THE MATCH

In a round cavern of glass, in steely water
(None yet so comfortless appalled the day)
A man-eel poised, his lacquer-skin disparted
In desert reds and wharfy green; his eyes too
Burned like beads of venom.
Beyond the glass the torturer stood, with thrustings,
Passes, grimaces, toothy grins, warped œillades.
To this black magic mania's eel retorted
With fierce yet futile muzzle, and lancing darted
In an electric rapine, against the wall
Of glass, or life: those disputants of nothing,
So acidly attracting, lovingly loathing,
Driven by cold radii, goblin lovers, seemed yet
The difficult dumb-show of my generation.

TOKYO 1926

from JAPANESE GARLAND *(1928)*

THE AUTHOR'S LAST WORDS TO HIS STUDENTS*

Forgive what I, adventuring highest themes,
    Have spoiled and darkened, and the awkward hand
That longed to point the moral of man's dreams
    But shut the wicket-gates of fairyland:
            So by too harsh intrusion
            Left colourless confusion.

*In the School of English Literature, at the Tokyo Imperial University, 1924-1927.

For even the glories that I most revered,
    Seen through my gloomed perspective in strange mood,
Were not what to our British seers appeared;
    I spoke of peace, I made a solitude,
        Herding with deathless graces
        My hobbling commonplaces.

Forgive that eyeless lethargy which chilled
    Your ardours and I fear dimmed much fine gold—
What your bright passion, leaping ages, thrilled
    To find and claim, and I yet dared withhold;
        These and all chance offences
        Against your finer senses.

And I will ever pray for your souls' health,
    Remembering how, deep-burdened, eager-eyed,
You loved imagination's commonwealth,
    Following with smiling wonder that frail guide
        Who hears beyond the ocean
        The voice of your devotion.

from **UNDERTONES OF WAR** *(1928)*

THE ZONNEBEKE ROAD

Morning, if this late withered light can claim
Some kindred with that merry flame
Which the young day was wont to fling through space!
Agony stares from each grey face,
And yet the day is come; stand down! stand down!
Your hands unclasp from rifles while you can;
The frost has pierced them to the bended bone?
Why, see old Stevens there, that iron man,
Melting the ice to shave his grotesque chin!
Go ask him, shall we win?
I never liked this bay, some foolish fear
Caught me the first time that I came in here;

That dugout fallen in awakes, perhaps,
Some formless haunting of some corpse's chaps.
True, and wherever we have held the line,
There were such corners, seeming-saturnine
For no good cause.
                              Now where Haymarket starts,
That is no place for soldiers with weak hearts;
The minenwerfers have it to the inch.
Look, how the snow-dust whisks along the road,
Piteous and silly; the stones themselves must flinch
In this east wind; the low sky like a load
Hangs over, a dead weight. But what a pain
Must gnaw where its clay cheek
Crushes the shell-chopped trees that fang the plain—
The ice-bound throat gulps out a gargoyle shriek.
The wretched wire before the village line
Rattles like rusty brambles or dead bine,
And then the daylight oozes into dun;
Black pillars, those are trees where roadways run.
Even Ypres now would warm our souls; fond fool,
Our tour's but one night old, seven more to cool!
O screaming dumbness, O dull clashing death,
Shreds of dead grass and willows, homes and men,
Watch as you will, men clench their chattering teeth
And freeze you back with that one hope, disdain.

CONCERT PARTY: BUSSEBOOM

The stage was set, the house was packed,
    The famous troop began;
Our laughter thundered, act by act;
    Time light as sunbeams ran.

Dance sprang and spun and neared and fled,
    Jest chirped at gayest pitch,
Rhythm dazzled, action sped
    Most comically rich.

With generals and lame privates both
    Such charms worked wonders, till

59

The show was over: lagging, loth
   We faced the sunset chill;

And standing on the sandy way,
   With the cracked church peering past,
We heard another matinée,
   We heard the maniac blast

Of barrage south by Saint Eloi,
   And the red lights flaming there
Called madness: Come, my bonny boy,
   And dance to the latest air.

To this new concert, white we stood;
   Cold certainty held our breath;
While men in the tunnels below Larch Wood
   Were kicking men to death.

VLAMERTINGHE:
Passing the Château, July 1917

'And all her silken flanks with garlands drest'—
But we are coming to the sacrifice.
Must those have flowers who are not yet gone West?
May those have flowers who live with death and lice?
This must be the floweriest place
That earth allows; the queenly face
Of the proud mansion borrows grace for grace
Spite of those brute guns lowing at the skies.

Bold great daisies' golden lights,
Bubbling roses' pinks and whites—
Such a gay carpet! poppies by the million;
Such damask! such vermilion!
But if you ask me, mate, the choice of colour
Is scarcely right; this red should have been duller.

GOUZEAUCOURT: THE DECEITFUL CALM

How unpurposed, how inconsequential
Seemed those southern lines when in the pallor
    Of the dying winter
    First we went there!

Grass thin-waving in the wind approached them,
Red roofs in the near view feigned survival,
    Lovely mockers, when we
    There took over.

There war's holiday seemed, nor though at known times
Gusts of flame and jingling steel descended
    On the bare tracks, would you
    Picture death there.

Snow or rime-frost made a solemn silence,
Bluish darkness wrapped in dangerous safety;
    Old hands thought of tidy
    Living-trenches!

There it was, my dears, that I departed,
Scarce a greater traitor ever! There too
    Many of you soon paid for
    That false mildness.

LA QUINQUE RUE

O road in dizzy moonlight bleak and blue,
With forlorn effigies of farms besprawled,
With trees bitterly bare or snapped in two,
Why riddle me thus—attracted and appalled?
For surely now the grounds both left and right
Are tilled, and scarless houses undismayed
Glow in the lustrous mercy of sweet night,
And one may hear the flute or fiddle played.
Why lead me then
Through the foul-gorged, the cemeterial fen
To fear's sharp sentries? Why do dreadful rags

Fur these bulged banks, and feebly move to the wind?
That battered drum, say why it clacks and brags?
Another and another! what's behind?
How is it that these flints flame out fire's tongue,
Shrivelling my thought? these collapsed skeletons,
What are they, and these iron hunks among?
Why clink those spades, why glare these startling suns
And topple to the wet and crawling grass,
Where the strange briars in taloned hedges twine?
What need of that stopped tread, that countersign?
O road, I know those muttering groups you pass.
I know those moments shrill as shivered glass;
But, I am told, to-night you safely shine
To trim roofs and cropped fields; the error's mine.

'TRENCH NOMENCLATURE'

Genius named them, as I live! What but genius could compress
In a title what man's humour said to man's supreme distress?
Jacob's Ladder ran reversed, from earth to a fiery pit extending
With not angels but poor Angles, those for the most part descending.
Thence *Brock's Benefit* commanded endless fireworks by two nations,
Yet some voices there were raised aginst the rival coruscations.
Picturedome peeped out upon a dream, not Turner could surpass,
And presently the picture moved, and greyed with corpses and morass.
So down south; and if remembrance travel north, she marvels yet
At the sharp Shakespearean names, and with sad mirth her eyes are wet.
The Great Wall of China rose, a four-foot breastwork, fronting guns
That, when the word dropped, beat at once its silly ounces with brute
     tons;
Odd *Krab Krawl* on paper looks, and odd the foul-breathed alley twisted,
As one feared to twist there too, if *Minnie*, forward quean, insisted.
Where the Yser at *Dead End* floated on its bloody waters
Dead and rotten monstrous fish, note (east) *The Pike and Eel* head-
     quarters.
Ah, such names and apparitions! name on name! what's in a name?
From the fabled vase the genie in his cloud of horror came.

FAMILIARITY

Dance not your spectral dance at me;
    I know you well!
Along this lane there lives no tree
    But I can tell.
I know each fall and rise and twist;
You—why, a wildflower in the mist,
    The moon, the mist.

Sound not that long alarm, gray tower,
    I know you well;
This is your habit at this hour,
    You and your bell!
If once, I heard a hundred times
Through evening's ambuscade your chimes—
    Dark tower, your chimes.

Enforce not that no-meaning so,
    Familiar stream;
Whether you tune it high or low,
    I know your theme;
A proud-fed but a puny rill,
A meadow brook, poured quick and shrill—
    Alone and shrill.

Sprawl not so monster-like, blind mist;
    I know not 'seems';
I am too old a realist
    To take sea-dreams
From you, or think a great white Whale
Floats through our hawthorn-scented vale—
    This foam-cold vale.

A SUNRISE IN MARCH

While on my cheek the sour and savage wind
Confuses soul with sense, while unamazed

I view the siege of pale-starred horror raised
By dawn whose waves charge stern and crimson-lined,
In cold blue tufts of battle-smoke afar,
And sable crouching thickets by my way—
While I thus droop, the living land grows gay
With starry welcomes to the conquering star!

From every look-out whence they watch him win
(That angry Cromwell!) high on thorn and bine
The selfless wildbirds hail their holy light:
With changes free as flute or violin,
To naked fields they peal as proud and fine
As though they had not dreamed of death all night.

THE KILN

Beside the creek where seldom oar or sail
Adventures, and the gulls whistling like men
Patrol the pasture of the falling tide,
Like Timon's mansion stands the silent kiln.
Half citadel, half temple, strong it stands
With layered stones built into cavernous curves,
The fire-vault now as cool as leaves and stones
And dews can be. Here came my flitting thought,
The only visitor of a sunny day,
Except the half-mad wasp that fights with all,
The leaping cricket in his apple-green,
And emerald beetle with his golden helmet;
While the south wind woke all the colony
Of sorrels and sparse daisies, berried ivies
And thorns bowed down with sloes, and brambles red
Offering a feast that no child came to take.

In these unwanted derelicts of man
Nature has touched the picture with a smile
Of more than usual mystery; the far heights
With thunderous forest marshalled are her toil,
But this her toy, her petty larceny
That pleased her, lurking like a gipsy girl,
My thought came here with artfulness like hers

To spy on her, and, though she fled, pursued
To where on eastern islands, in the cells
Of once grave seers, her iris woos the wind.

THE CORRELATION

Again the yellow dusk or light along
The winter hills: again the trees' black claws
Waiting and working by the bridge of space:
Again the tower, among tombs a huge tomb;
White scattered birds, a black horse in the meads,
And the eel-track of the brown stream fringing by.

Would understanding win herself my vote,
Now, having known this crisis thirty years,
She should decide me why it overwhelms
My chart of time and history; should declare
What in the spirit of a man long schooled
To human concept and devotion dear,
Upraised by sure example, undefiled
By misery and defeat, still in the sun—
What stirs him, and finds its brother-self,
From that late sky. Again the sky, that tower,
These effigies and wizardries of chance,
Those soundless vollies of pale and distant birds
Have taken him, and from his whirring toils
Made him as far away, as unconcerned,
As consonant with the Power as its bare trees.

THE DEEPER FRIENDSHIP

Were all eyes changed, were even poetry cold,
Were those long systems of hope that I tried to deploy
Skeletons, still I should keep one final hold,
Since clearer and clearer returns my first-found joy.

I would go, once more, through the sunless autumn in trouble;
Thin and cold rain dripping down through branches black,
Streams hoarse-hurrying and pools spreading over the stubble,
And the waggoner leaving the hovel under his sack

Would guide me along by the gate and deserted siding,
The inn with the tattered arbour, the choking weir;
And yet, security there would need small guiding.
I know one hearth, one love that shine beyond fear.

There, though the sharpest storm and flood were abroad,
And the last husk and leaf were stripped from the tree,
I would sue for peace where the rats and mice have gnawed,
And well content that Nature should bury me.

THE BLIND LEAD THE BLIND

Dim stars like snowflakes are fluttering in heaven,
Down the cloud-mountains by wind-torrents riven;
There are still chances, but one more than all
Slowly burns out on the sea's dark wall—
      The best ever given.

One, the divinest, goes down to the dark,
In a red sullen vanishing, a poor stifled spark.
You, who have reason, were staring at this
As though by your gaze it would clear the abyss—
      It was once your sea-mark.

Here on the shore too the sighed monotones
Of waves that in weakness slip past the purled stones;
The seethe of blown sand round the dry fractured hull,
Salt-reeds and tusked fence; hear the struck gull
      With death in his bones.

Slow comes the net in, that's filled with frustration;
Night ends the day of thwart discreation;
I would be your miracle-worker, sad friend,
Bid a music for you and a new star ascend,—
      But I know isolation.

REPORT ON EXPERIENCE

I have been young, and now am not too old;
And I have seen the righteous forsaken,
His health, his honour and his quality taken.
        This is not what we were formerly told.

I have seen a green country, useful to the race,
Knocked silly with guns and mines, its villages vanished,
Even the last rat and the last kestrel banished—
        God bless us all, this was peculiar grace.

I knew Seraphina; Nature gave her hue,
Glance, sympathy, note, like one from Eden.
I saw her smile warp, heard her lyric deaden;
        She turned to harlotry;—this I took to be new.

Say what you will, our God sees how they run.
These disillusions are His curious proving
That He loves humanity and will go on loving;
        Over there are faith, life, virtue in the sun.

A CONNOISSEUR

Presume not that gray idol with the scythe
And hourglass of the stern perpetual sands
To be a mere insensate mill of hours,
Unawed by battles, unbeguiled with flowers;
Think, this old Merlin may be vexed or blithe,
And for the future stretches hungry hands.

No last year's bride discovers more caprice
Than this bald magpie smuggling up his wit,
And in his crumbling belfry, where the cost
Of high-born death in plundered ruin's lost,
Nodding his glory to each glittering piece
Of glass or jewel that his fancy hit.

Close in the shop of some lean artizan,
Who carves a snuff-box for Squire Harkaway,

Time stoops, and stares, and knows his destined prize:
Croesus shall hunt this modest merchandize
When frieze and pillar of a master's plan
Are crushed in waggon-tracks to bind the clay.

There stalled theology makes angels weep
In twenty volumes blazoned red and gold,
And there a broadside's bawled about the street;
Time fetched his halfpence out and bought a sheet.
The twenty volumes slumber in a heap,
The ballad among heirlooms lives enrolled.

Lordly oration thronged the sculptured roof,
And pamphleteered in plaudits through the town;
The charlatan proclaimed his draughts and pills,
And tossed the crowd his woodcuts and his bills;
From rhetoric's remains Time flies aloof,
And hears the quack still pattering to the clown.

Voluptuous canvas! Venus in May-bloom,
Sunshine of vital gold, faun-twinkling groves,
Harmonious limbs and volant veils, go mourn;
For you will lie with fire, while Time has borne
The blue-daubed frigate from the servants' room
To swell the mad collection of his loves.

VALUES

Till darkness lays a hand on these gray eyes
And out of man my ghost is sent alone,
It is my chance to know that force and size
Are nothing but by answered undertone.
No beauty even of absolute perfection
Dominates here—the glance, the pause, the guess
Must be my amulets of resurrection;
Raindrops may murder, lightnings may caress.

There I was tortured, but I cannot grieve;
There crowned and palaced—visibles deceive.
That storm of belfried cities in my mind

Leaves me my vespers cool and eglantined.
From love's wide-flowering mountain-side I chose
The sprig of green, in which an angel shows.

from **THE POEMS** *(1930)*

'TRANSPORT UP' AT YPRES

The thoroughfares that seem so dead to daylight passers-by
Change character when the dark comes down, and traffic starts to ply;
Never a noisier street than the Rue de Malou then becomes
With the cartwheels jolting the dead awake, and the cars like rumbling
    drums.

The crazy houses watch them pass, and stammer with the roar,
The drivers hustle on their mules, more come behind and more;
Briskly the black mules clatter by, to-day was Devil's Mass;
The loathly smell of picric here, and there a touch of gas.

From silhouettes to pitchy blur, beneath the bitter stars,
The interminable convoy streams of horses, vans and cars.
They clamour through the cheerless night, the streets a slattern maze,
The sentries at the corners shout them on their different ways.

And so they go, night after night, and chance the shrapnel fire,
The sappers' waggons stowed with frames and concertina wire,
The ration-limbers for the line, the lorries for the guns:
While overhead with fleering light stare down those withered suns.

PREMATURE REJOICING

What's that over there?
                Thiepval Wood.
Take a steady look at it; it'll do you good.
Here, these glasses will help you. See any flowers?
There sleeps Titania (correct—the Wood is ours);
There sleeps Titania in a deep dugout,

Waking, she wonders what all the din's about,
And smiles through her tears, and looks ahead ten years,
And sees her Wood again, and her usual Grenadiers,

    All in green,
    Music in the moon;
  The burnt rubbish you've just seen
  Won't beat the Fairy Queen;
    All the same, it's a shade too soon
    For you to scribble rhymes
    In your army book
    About those times;
    Take another look;
  That's where the difficulty is, over there.

TO JOY

Is not this enough for moan
To see this babe all motherless—
A babe beloved—thrust out alone
    Upon death's wilderness?
Our tears fall, fall, fall—I would weep
My blood away to make her warm,
Who never went on earth one step,
    Nor heard the breath of the storm.
How shall you go, my little child,
Alone on that most wintry wild?

A JAPANESE EVENING

Round us the pines are darkness
That with a wild melodious piping rings
While in the ditches
Slow as toads in English gardens
The little landcrabs move.
We re-discover our path,
And, coming to the cottage, are greeted
With hierophantic usherings and oracles,
And a grin behind the screen, I imagine.
We guess full fathom five, and take up the chopsticks.

The metal-blue cucumber slices,
Rice, string beans,
And green tea over,
The housekeeper looking kindly amazement
At the master of the house
Soon makes all shipshape.
After all, they possess an American clock,
A very fine, a high-collar clock.
She sits on the mat, awaiting the next oddity.

Lanterns moon the outer darkness,
And merrily in come floating
(So gently they foot the honourable straw)
Three young girls, who sit them down.
A conference;
Almost the Versailles of the Far East:
The master, beaming,
His white hair in the lamplight seeming brighter with his pleasure,
Asks me what I call *O tsuki sama*.
Moon.
Mooon.
Moon.
He has got it; right first time,
But not the next.
Moooni.
(The housekeeper cannot suppress her giggles,
Okashii, she says, and so it is.)
We now pass naturally to the
Electric Light.
But he will not have that,
There are no things like that in heaven and earth
In his philology.
I repeat—what I said;
He repeats—what he said.
We close at Erecturiku Rightu.
We fasten also on:
The cat, who becomes catsu,
The dog, who proceeds doggi,
(And I suspect has rabies beginning):
Himself, O-Ji-San, Orudu Genturuman,
And all sorts of enigmas.

The girls are quicker, more nimble-throated,
And will reproduce exactly the word, but he lays the law down;
Having re-orientated Fan,
Which they pronounced Fan,
Into Weino,
He instructs them how it ought to be pronounced,
Obediently young Japan reiterates his decision,
Not without an ocular hint to the stranger
That they have concealed the other rendering in their minds . . .
I hear their voices tinkling, lessening
Over the firefly grass,
Along the seething sand below the pines,
At the end of the entertainment.

UNDER A THOUSAND WORDS

'A thousand words on Courage.'—This request
Dropped on me like a bomb on a sandbag shelter,
And after much vague mental repetition
Ranging from La Boisselle to Lord Macaulay,
And metaphysical cross-examination
On memories of conspicuous gallant conduct,
I gave it up.
                    That afternoon our boat
Touched on a mud-flat, which we chose to cross,
And as we waddled through it, a three-inch crab
Disputed progress; one of his arms was gone;
The other he held ready like a boxer,
And backed and sidled to our every movement,
His one arm ready; and to command full view
Of the two monsters who had crossed the frontier,
He strained his body backward, and stood tilted,
Parrying every stroke we acted at him,
Eyeing us, holding the line.
                    'But you call this Instinct.'

THE SUNLIT VALE

I saw the sunlit vale, and the pastoral fairy-tale;
The sweet and bitter scent of the may drifted by;
And never have I seen such a bright bewildering green,
    But it looked like a lie,
    Like a kindly meant lie.

When gods are in dispute, one a Sidney, one a brute,
It would seem that human sense might not know, might not spy;
But though nature smile and feign where foul play has stabbed and slain,
    There's a witness, an eye,
    Nor will charms blind that eye.

Nymph of the upland song and the sparkling leafage young,
For your merciful desire with these charms to beguile,
For ever be adored; muses yield you rich reward;
    But you fail, though you smile—
    That other does not smile.

from **TO THEMIS** *(1931)*

INCIDENT IN HYDE PARK, 1803

The impulses of April, the rain-gems, the rose-cloud,
The frilling of flowers in the westering love-wind!
And here through the Park come gentlemen riding,
And there through the Park come gentlemen riding,
And behind the glossy horses Newfoundland dogs follow.
Says one dog to the other, 'This park, sir, is mine, sir.'
The reply is not wanting; hoarse clashing and mouthing
Arouses the masters.
Then Colonel Montgomery, of the Life-Guards, dismounts.
'Whose dog is this?' The reply is not wanting,
From Captain Macnamara, Royal Navy: 'My dog.'
'Then call your dog off, or by God he'll go sprawling.'
'If my dog goes sprawling, you must knock me down after.'
'Your name?' 'Macnamara, and yours is—' 'Montgomery.'

73

'And why, sir, not call your dog off?' 'Sir, I chose
Not to do so, no man has dictated to me yet,
And you, I propose, will not change that.' 'This place,
For adjusting disputes, is not proper'—and the Colonel,
Back to the saddle, continues, 'If your dog
Fights my dog, I warn you, I knock your dog down.
For the rest, you are welcome to know where to find me,
Colonel Montgomery; and you will of course
Respond with the due information.' 'Be sure of it.'

Now comes the evening, green-twinkling, clear-echoing,
And out to Chalk-farm the Colonel, the Captain,
Each with his group of believers, have driven.
>   Primrose Hill on an April evening
>   Even now in a fevered London
>   Sings a vesper sweet; but these
>   Will try another music. Hark!
These are the pistols; let us test them; quite perfect.
Montgomery, Macnamara six paces, two faces;
Montgomery, Macnamara—both speaking together
In nitre and lead, the style is incisive,
Montgomery fallen, Macnamara half-falling,
The surgeon exploring the work of the evening—
And the Newfoundland dogs stretched at home in the firelight.

The coroner's inquest; the view of one body;
And then, pale, supported, appears at Old Bailey
James Macnamara, to whom this arraignment:
>   You stand charged
>   That you
>   With force and arms
>   Did assault Robert Montgomery,
>   With a certain pistol
>   Of the value of ten shillings,
>   Loaded with powder and a leaden bullet,
>   Which the gunpowder, feloniously exploded,
>   Drove into the body of Robert Montgomery,
>   And gave
>   One mortal wound;
>   Thus you did kill and slay
>   The said Robert Montgomery.

74

O heavy imputation! O dead that yet speaks!
   O evening transparency, burst to red thunder!

Speak, Macnamara. He, tremulous as a windflower
Exactly imparts what had slaughtered the Colonel.
'Insignificant the origin of the fact before you;
Defending our dogs, we grew warm; that was nature;
That heat of itself had not led to disaster.
From defence to defiance was the leap that destroyed.
At once he would have at my deity, Honour—
"If you are offended you know where to find me."
On one side, I saw the wide mouths of Contempt,
Mouth to mouth working, a thousand vile gun-mouths;
On the other my Honour; Gentlemen of the Jury,
I am a Captain in the British Navy.'

Then said Lord Hood: 'For Captain Macnamara,
He is a gentleman and so says the Navy.'
Then said Lord Nelson: 'I have known Macnamara
Nine years, a gentleman, beloved in the Navy,
Not to be affronted by any man, true,
Yet as I stand here before God and my country,
Macnamara has never offended, and would not,
Man, woman, child.' Then a volley of admirals,
Almost Neptune in person, proclaim Macnamara
Mild, amiable, cautious, as any in the Navy;
And Mr Garrow rises, to state that if need be,
To assert the even temper and peace of his client,
He would call half the Captains in the British Navy.

Now we are shut from the duel that Honour
Must fight with the Law; no eye can perceive
The fields wherein hundreds of shadowy combats
Must decide between a ghost and a living idolon—
A ghost with his army of the terrors of bloodshed,
A half-ghost with the grand fleet of names that like sunrise
Have dazzled the race with their march on the ocean.

Twenty minutes. How say you?
               Not guilty.

Then from his chair with his surgeon the Captain
Walks home to his dog, his friends' acclamations
Supplying some colour to the pale looks he had,
Less pale than Montgomery's; and Honour rides on.

THE KISS

I am for the woods against the world,
    But are the woods for me?
I have sought them sadly, fearing
    My fate's mutability,
Or that which action and process make
    Of former sympathy.

Strange that those should arrive strangers
    Who were once entirely at home.
Colonnade, sunny wall and warren,
    Islet, osier, foam,
Buds and leaves and selves seemed
    Safe to the day of doom.

By-roads following, and this way wondering,
    I spy men abroad
In orchards, knarred and woody men
    Whose touch is bough and bud;
Co-arboreal sons of landscape.
    Then in the windstript wood

Is the cracking of stems; and under the thorn
    With a kobold's closeness lurks
The wanderer with his knife and rods,
    That like a bald rook works;
His woman-rook about the thicket
    Prowls at the hazel-forks.

Sheep lying out by the swollen river
    Let the flood roll down
Without so much as a glance; they know it;
    The hurling seas of brown
Cannot persuade the ferrying moorhen
    Her one willow will drown.

This way wondering, I renew
    Some sense of common right;
And through my armour of imposition
    Win the Spring's keen light,
Till for the woods against the world
    I kiss the aconite.

THE RECOVERY

From the dark mood's control
    I free my limbs; there's light still in the West.
The most virtuous, chaste, melodious soul
    Never was better blest.

Here medicine for the mind
    Lies in a gilded shade; this feather stirs
And my faith lives; the touch of this tree's rind,—
    And temperate sense recurs.

No longer the loud pursuit
    Of self-made clamour dulls the ear; here dwell
Twilight societies, twig, fungus, root,
    Soundless, and speaking well.

Beneath the accustomed dome
    Of this chance-planted, many-centuried tree
The snake-marked earthly multitudes are come
    To breathe their hour like me.

The leaf comes curling down,
    Another and another, gleam on gleam;
Above, celestial leafage glistens on,
    Borne by time's blue stream.

The meadow-stream will serve
    For my refreshment; that high glory yields
Imaginings that slay; the safe paths curve
    Through unexalted fields

Like these, where now no more
    My early angels walk and call and fly,

77

But the mouse stays his nibbling, to explore
   My eye with his bright eye.

A NIGHT-PIECE
From the Greek of Alcman

'Asleep; the pinnacles and the precipices of the mountains,
Headlands, and torrents, and all that walk and creep
On the shadowy earth that breeds them; the beasts that haunt in the
    mountains,
The world of bees, the kraken in the blue deep;
Even the orders of birds of widest wing are asleep.'

from **HALFWAY HOUSE** *(1932)*

THE MEMORIAL, 1914-1918

Against this lantern, shrill, alone
The wind springs out of the plain.
Such winds as this must fly and moan
Round the summit of every stone
On every hill; and yet a strain
Beyond the measure elsewhere known
Seems here.
       Who cries? who mingles with the gale?
Whose touch, so anxious and so weak, invents
A coldness in the coldness? in this veil
Of whirling mist what hue of clay consents?
Can atoms intercede?

And are those shafted bold constructions there,
Mines more than golden, wheels that outrace need,
Crowded coróns, victorious chimneys—are
Those touched with question too? pale with the dream
Of those who in this æther-stream
Are urging yet their painful, woundful theme?

Day flutters as a curtain, stirred
By a hidden hand; the eye grows blurred.
Those towers, uncrystalled, fade.
The wind from north and east and south
Comes with its starved white mouth
And at this crowning trophy cannot rest—
No, speaks as something past plain words distressed.

Be still, if these your voices are; this monolith
For you and your high sleep was made.
Some have had less.
No gratitude in deathlessness?
No comprehension of the tribute paid?

You would speak still? Who with?

NOVEMBER 1, 1931

We talked of ghosts; and I was still alive;
And I that very day was thirty-five;
Alone once more, I stared about my room
And wished some ghost would be a friend and come;
I cared not of what shape or semblance; terror
Was nothing in comparison with error;
I wished some ghost would come, to talk of fate,
And tell me why I drove my pen so late,
And help with observations on my knack
Of being always on the bivouac,
Here and elsewhere, for ever changing ground,
Finding and straightway losing what I found,
Baffled in time, fumbling each sequent date,
Mistaking Magdalen for the Menin Gate.
That much I saw without transmortal talk,
That war had ended my sublunar walk—
Forgive me, dear, honoured and saintly friends;
Ingratitude suspect not; this transcends.
Forgive, O sweet red-smiling love, forgive,
If this is life, for your delight I live;
How every lamp, how every pavement flames
Your beauty at me, and your faith acclaims!

But from my silences your kindness grew,
And I surrendered for the time to you,
And still I hold you glorious and my own,
I'd take your hands, your lips; but I'm alone.
So I was forced elsewhere, and would accost
For colloquy and guidance some kind ghost.
As one that with a serious trust was sent
Afar, and bandits seized him while he went,
And long delayed, so I; I yearned to catch
What I should know before my grave dispatch
Was to be laid before that General
Who in a new Time cries 'backs to the wall'.
No ghost was granted me; and I must face
Uncoached the masters of that Time and Space,
And there with downcast murmurings set out
What my gross late appearance was about.

from **CHOICE OR CHANCE** *(1934)*

THE SURPRISE

Shot from the zenith of desire
    Some faultless beams found where I lay,
Not much expecting such white fire
    Across a slow close working-day.

What a great song then sang the brook,
    The fallen pillar's grace how new;
The vast white oaks like cowslips shook—
    And I was winged, and flew to you.

THE COTTAGE AT CHIGASAKI

That well you drew from is the coldest drink
In all the country Fuji looks upon;
And me, I never come to it but I think
The poet lived here once who one hot noon
Came dry and eager, and with wonder saw

80

The morning-glory* about the bucket twined,
Then with a holy heart went out to draw
His gallon where he might; the poem's signed
By him and Nature. We need not retire,
But freely dip, and wash away the salt
And sand we've carried from the sea's blue fire;
Discuss a melon; and without great fault,
Though comfort is not poetry's best friend,
We'll write a poem too, and sleep at the end.

*Perhaps the most familiar Japanese poem is that which says, approximately, 'The morning-glory has taken hold of the well-bucket; I'll borrow some water elsewhere.'

THE BRANCH LINE

Professing loud energy, out of the junction departed
The branch-line engine. The small train rounded the bend
Watched by us pilgrims of summer, and most by me,—
Who had known this picture since first my travelling started,
And knew it as sadly pleasant, the usual end
Of singing returns to beloved simplicity.

The small train went from view behind the plantation,
Monotonous,—but there's a grace in monotony!
I felt its journey, I watched in imagination
Its brown smoke spun with sunshine wandering free
Past the great weir with its round flood-mirror beneath,
And where the magpie rises from orchard shadows,
And among the oasts, and like a rosy wreath
Mimicking children's flower-play in the meadows.

The thing so easy, so daily, of so small stature
Gave me another picture: of war's warped face
Where still the sun and the leaf and the lark praised Nature,
But no little engine bustled from place to place;
Then summer succeeded summer, yet only ghosts
Or to-morrow's ghosts could venture hand or foot
In the track between the terrible telegraph-posts,—
The end of all things lying between the hut
Which lurked this side, and the shattered local train
That.
    So easy it was; and should that come again—.

81

AT RUGMER

Among sequestered farms and where brown orchards
Weave in the thin and coiling wind, and where
The pale cold river ripples still as moorhens
Work their restless crossing,
Among such places, when October warnings
Sound from each kex and thorn and shifting leaf,
We well might wander, and renew some stories
Of a dim time when we were kex and thorn,
Sere leaf, ready to hear a hissing wind
Whip down and wipe us out; our season seemed
At any second closing.
So, we were wrong. But we have lived this landscape,
And have an understanding with these shades.

AN OMINOUS VICTORIAN

I am the *Poems of* the late *Eliza Cook*,
For sixty odd years I have occupied this nook;
I remember myself as a bright young book
       On a bookseller's ormolu table.

Just beside me I had quite a nice friend,
Mrs. Heman's Works, and at the far end
Was one called *It's Never Too Late to Mend*,
       And a print of the Tower of Babel.

We were a pretty pair, *Mrs. H.* and I,
My crimson velvet was the best you could buy;
She wore green—and a love of a tie,—
       I suppose it would now look tawdry.

One fine morning she was taken, as I heard,
For a prize to a Miss Georgiana Bird.
Then my turn came—I'd to carry the word
       Of 'Podgers, with love to Audrey.'

Some little time I was much in request,
Either she read me or hugged me to her breast,

And several sorts of ferns were pressed
    Between my red-ruled pages.

O if only I could warn some of you young books,
Who are taken in like me by loving looks,
—There was no name then like *Eliza Cook's*;
    It's preparedness that assuages.

Then, one night (I can almost see it still)
A letter came; she put down her quill,
And read, and stormed, 'I should like to kill
    That two-faced miscreant Podgers';

And she flung me under the settee, where
I lay in want of light and air,
Enduring the supercilious stare
    Of the *Works of Samuel Rogers*

That always stood on the bracket—well,
There's not much really left to tell,
I was rescued by the housemaid Nell
    Who hadn't no time for reading,

But on the whatnot made me do
For a lamp (of the horridest butcher-blue)
To stand on; and she shrouded me, too,
    In a mat of her mother's beading.

And here I am, and yet I suppose
I'd better not grumble, as this world goes,
For I see I'm outstaying rows and rows
    Of the newest immortal fiction;

And *Rogers* has vanished—I don't know where—
With his *Pleasures of Memory*—and I don't care;
I presume he's propping the leg of a chair
    With his sniffy elegant diction.

LATE LIGHT

Come to me where the swelling wind assails the wood with a sea-like roar,
While the yellow west is still afire; come borne by the wind up the hill-
     side track;
  There is quiet yet, and brightness more
  Than day's clear fountains to noon rayed back
     If you will come;

  If you will come, and against this fall
  Of leaves and light and what seemed time,
  Now changed to haste, against them all
  Glow, calm and young; O help me climb
  Above the entangling phantoms harrying
  Shaken ripeness, unsighted prime;
  Come unwithering and unvarying—
  Tell claw-handed Decline to scrawl
  A million menaces on the wall
  For whom it will; while safe we two
  Move where no knife-gust ever blew,
  And no boughs crack, and no bells toll,
  Through the tempest's ominous interval,
     Penitential low recall.

WRITING A SKETCH OF A FORGOTTEN POET

Here this great summer day,
  While the fields are wild
With flowers you name, I stay,
  And have learnedly compiled

From shaky books, too few,
  Dry registers,
Something of the living you;
  And have gleaned your verse.

You might have laughed to see,
  With this rich sun,

One pent in a library
    Who else might run

Free in the flashing sweet
    Life-lavishing air.
Or, lover of books, you'd greet
    Such constancy and care.

You might have laughed to hear
    Your stanzas read—
If it were not so clear
    The dead are dead.

What gulfs between us lie!
    I had thought them crossed,
Dreaming to gratify
    Your unimpatient ghost.

IN MY TIME

Touched with a certain silver light
In each man's retrospection,
There are important hours; some others
Seem to grow kingfisher's feathers,
Or glow like sunflowers; my affection
In the first kind finds more delight.

I would not challenge you to discover
Finally why you dwell
In this ward or that of your experience.
Men may vary without variance.
Each vase knows the note, the bell,
Which thrills it like a lover.

When I am silent, when a distance
Dims my response, forgive;
Accept that when the past has beckoned,
There is no help; all else comes second;
Agree, the way to live
Is not to dissect existence.

All the more waive common reason
If the passion when revealed
Seem of poor blood; if the silver hour
Be nothing but an uncouth, shot-torn tower,
And a column crossing a field,
Bowed men, to a dead horizon.

'CAN YOU REMEMBER?'

Yes, I still remember
    The whole thing in a way;
Edge and exactitude
    Depend on the day.

Of all that prodigious scene
    There seems scanty loss,
Though mists mainly float and screen
    Canal, spire and fosse;

Though commonly I fail to name
    That once obvious Hill,
And where we went and whence we came
    To be killed, or kill.

Those mists are spiritual
    And luminous-obscure,
Evolved of countless circumstance
    Of which I am sure;

Of which, at the instance
    Of sound, smell, change and stir,
New-old shapes for ever
    Intensely recur.

And some are sparkling, laughing, singing,
    Young, heroic, mild;
And some incurable, twisted,
    Shrieking, dumb, defiled.

ON A PICTURE BY DÜRER
Sonnenuntergang

Where found you, Dürer, that strange group of trees,
That seared, shamed, mutilated group still standing
To tell us *This is War*: where found you these?
I did not guess, when last I saw shells landing
Smash on the track beside, how old they were.
They had been good tall pines, I saw, but not
Of such great bole as argued they stood there
When your antiquity might pass the spot.

A thousand of us who as yet survive
From what was modern war the other day
Could recognize them, killed in the great Drive
Which strewed so many bones in glory's way.
But, you, your date was wrong. From which of your towers
Saw you that night across the centuries,
Under that cloud with baleful eye slits, ours—
Our sign, our shape, our dumb but eloquent trees?

CRICKET, I CONFESS

'Sir, I cannot profess to understand
One thing in England'—and Sakabé scanned
My face to be sure there was no offence astir,—
'It is Cricket, I confess. In the English character
That's the chief puzzle I have.' ' "My horn is dry,"
If you don't understand it, no more do I.'
Far out in the valley the sun was gilding green
Those meadows which in England most are seen,
Where churchyard, church, inn, forge and loft stand round
With cottages, and through the ages bound
The duckpond, and the stocks, and cricket-ground.
And I fell silent, while kind memories played
Bat and ball in the sunny past, not much dismayed
Why these things were, and why I liked them so.
O my Relf and Jessop and Hutchings long ago.

TO W. O. AND HIS KIND

If even you, so able and so keen,
And master of the business you reported
Seem now almost as though you had never been,
And in your simple purpose nearly thwarted,
What hope is there? What harvest from those hours
Deliberately, and in the name of truth,
Endured by you? Your witness moves no Powers,
And younger youth resents your sentient youth.

You would have stayed me with some parable,
The grain of mustard seed, the boy that thrust
His arm into the leaking dike to quell
The North Sea's onrush. Would you were not dust.
With you I might invent, and make men try,
Some kindly shelter from this frantic sky.

from POEMS 1930-1940 *(1941)*

A NOT UNUSUAL CASE

It may be so: their love was never fire,
Never 'a wonder and a wild desire,'
    What brought them first together?
          What 'come hither'?
And what does that concern us now, or them?
Now, though life's whole vast various multitude
Were at their choice, and Venus wildly wooed
    With every stratagem,
          I still conclude
They would not alter much, nor dally far.
They, happiest in not following some queer star,
On usual roads, by frequent course, combined,
Are one, they mean one; them no tragic find,
Caprice, inversion, egotism shall break.
They are as children at the same good table,

Whom wisdom plenishes; whether bread or cake,
It is their common lot; not all are able
To count on daily sustenance; and this
Regular through long years is better bliss
Than chancing kickshaws. So, I guess, they live.
I wonder when it happened, their last kiss;
But maybe more than any kiss can give
Dwells in their composition: smile who will,
They thread the maze that baffles beauty still.

THE SUM OF ALL

So rise, enchanting haunting faithful
Music of life recalled and now revealing
Unity; now discerned beyond
Fear, obscureness, casualty,
Exhaustion, shame and wreck,
As what was best,
As what was deeply well designed.
So rise, as a clear hill road with steady ascension,
Issuing from drifted outskirts, huddled houses,
Casual inns where guests may enter and wait
Many a moment till the hostess find them;
Thence ever before the carter, passing the quarries,
The griffin-headed gateways,
Windmill, splashing rill, derelict sheepfold,
Tower of a thousand years—
Through the pinewoods,
Where warm stones lodge the rose-leaf butterfly;
Crossing the artillery ranges whose fierce signs
Mean nothing now, whose gougings look like
Bird-baths now; and last, the frontier farm
And guard-house made of bracken.
Rising to this old eyrie, quietly forsaken,
You bear me on, and not me only.
All difference sheds away,
All shrivelling of the sense, anxious prolepsis,
Injury, staring suspicion,
Fades into pure and wise advance.
So rise; so let me pass.

WHAT IS WINTER?

The haze upon the meadow
        Denies the dying year,
For the sun's within it, something bridal
        Is more than dreaming here.
There is no end, no severance,
No moment of deliverance,
                No quietus made,
Though quiet abounds and deliverance moves
                In that sunny shade.

What is winter? a word,
        A figure, a clever guess.
That time-word does not answer to
        This drowsy wakefulness.
The secret stream scorns interval
Though the calendar shouts one from the wall;
        The spirit has no last days;
And death is no more dead than this
        Flower-haunted haze.

TIMBER

In the avenues of yesterday
A tree might have a thing to say.
        Horsemen then heard
        From the branches a word
That sent them serious on their way.

A tree,—a beam, a box, a crutch,
Costing so little or so much;
        Wainscot or stair,
        Barge, baby's chair,
A pier, a flute, a mill, a hutch.

That tree uprooted lying there
Will make such things with knack and care,

Unless you hear
From its boughs too clear
The word that has whitened the traveller's hair.

A PROSPECT OF SWANS

Walking the river way to change our note
From the hard season and from harder care,
        Marvelling we found the swans,
The swans on sullen swollen dykes afloat
Or moored on tussocks, a full company there,
White breasts and necks, advance and poise and stir
Filling the scene, while rays of steel and bronze
From the far dying sun touched the dead reeds.

So easy was the manner of each one,
So sure and wise the course of all their needs,
So free their unity, in that level sun
And floodland tipped with sedge and osiery,
It might have been where man was yet to be,
Some mere where none but swans were ever kings,
Where gulls might hunt, a wide flight in from sea,
And page-like small birds come: all innocent wings.

O picture of some first divine intent,
O young world which perhaps was modelled thus,
        Where even hard winter meant
No disproportion, hopeless hungers none,
And set no task which could not well be done.
Now this primeval pattern gleamed at us
Right near the town's black smoke-towers and the roar
Of trains bearing the sons of man to war.

THOUGHTS OF THOMAS HARDY

'Are you looking for someone, you who come pattering
Along the empty corridor, dead leaf, to my door,
And before I had noticed the leaves were now dying?'

91

'No, nobody; but the way was open.
The wind blew that way.
There was no other way.
And why your question?'

'O, I felt I saw someone with forehead bent downward
At the sound of your coming,
And he in that sound
Looked aware of a vaster threne of decline,
And considering a law of all life.
Yet he lingered, one lovingly regarding
Your particular fate and experience, poor leaf.'

THE VANISHING LAND

Flashing far, tolling sweet, telling of a city fine
The steeple cons the country round, and signals farm and kiln and mine,
Inns by the road are each one good, the carters here are friendly men,
And this is a country where I mean to come again and come again.
There was a child, though, last time I was passing by St. Hubert shrine,
A child whose torn black frock and thin white cheek in memory brighter
    shine
Than abeles and than spires. I said, I pledge this blossom's better growth,
And so began, but one day failed; what sightless hours, and busy sloth
Followed, and now the child is lost, and no voice comes on any wind;
The silver spire gets farther off, and the inns are difficult to find.

from AFTER THE BOMBING & OTHER SHORT POEMS (1949)

THE TREE IN THE GOODS YARD

So sigh, that hearkening pasts arouse
In the magic circle of your boughs,—
So timelessly, on sound's deep sea,
Sail your unfurled melody,
        My small dark Tree.

Who set you in this smoky yard
None tells me; it might seem too hard

A fate for a tree whose place should be
With a sounding proud-plumed company
       By a glittering sea.

And yet you live with liking here,
Are well, have some brocade to wear,
And solitary, mysteriously
Revoice light airs as sighs, which free
       Tombed worlds for me.

AFTER THE BOMBING

My hesitant design it was, in a time when no man feared,
To make a poem on the last poor flower to have grown on the patch of
   land
Where since a gray enormous stack of shops and offices reared
Its bulk as though to eternity there to stand.

Moreover I dreamed of a lyrical verse to welcome another flower,
The first to blow on the hidden site when the concrete block should cease
Gorging the space; it could not be mine to foretell the means, the hour,
But nature whispered something of a longer lease.

We look from the street now over a breezy wilderness of bloom,
Now, crowding its colours between the sills and cellars, hosts of flame
And foam, pearl-pink and thunder-red, befriending the makeshift tomb
Of a most ingenious but impermanent claim.

FROM THE FLYING-BOAT

Into the blue undisturbable main
    The blue streams flow,
    In time they flow
Out of chasms vaporous, spurs far-whitening, winding gorges
    Woven of snow;
    This height we gain.
    The country enlarges.

There the mountain cloudland, and far at the verge
    Cliff-cloudlands upsurge;

Here, countless, an archipelago—
How the islands tower in their strength, quincunxes so
May confront such eyes as understand them, down below;

And yet up here I hardly know,
So little is this brilliant change, although
It extends in kingdom bright, so fast we go
Into apparent eternity—but, truth is, all things flow.

And now I am mounted aloft and have taken a wing,
Into the blue undisturbable oceaning,
More prospect than pyramidal Egypt, or perhaps the Mountains of the
    Moon could bring,
        With whom shall we meet in this place?
        Why hides He His face?

THE HALTED BATTALION

One hour from far returns: Each man we had
Was well content that hour, the time, the place,
And war's reprieve combining. Each good face
Stood easy, and announced life not too bad.

Then almost holy came a light, a sense,
And whence it came I did not then inquire;
Simple the secne,—a château wall, a spire,
Towpath, swing-bridge, canal with bulrush-fence.

Still I, as dreamer known, that morning saw
The others round me taken with a dream.
I wondered since that never one of them
Recalls it; but how should they? We who draw
Picture and meaning are the dreamless, we
Are sentinels of time while the rest are free.

HIGH ELMS, BRACKNELL

Two buds we took from thousands more
    In Shelley's garden overgrown,

Beneath our roof they are now full-blown,
A royal pair, a scarlet twain
    Through whose warm lives our thoughts explore
    Back through long years to come at one
Which Shelley loved in sun or rain.

Fleeting's the life of these strange flowers,
    Enchanting poppies satin-frilled,
    Dark-purple hearts, yet these rebuild
A distant world, a summer dead*
    Millions of poppy-lives ere ours,
    And Shelley's visionary towers
Come nearer in their Indian red;

Not but some shadow of despair
    In this dark purple ominous
    From that high summer beckons us;
And such a shadow, such a doom
    Was lurking in the garden there.
    We could not name the incubus,
Save that it haunted Shelley's home.

Was it that through the same glass door
    With weary heart, uncertain why,
    But first discerning love can die,
Harriet had moved alone and slow;
    Or Shelley in the moonlight bore
    The cold curt word Necessity
From poppies that had seemed to know?

Then tracing the lost path between
    The herbs and flowers and wilderness,
    Whose was the phantom of our guess
Drawn by that quiet deserted pond
    With little boat, now scarcely seen
    For tears or bodings? Whose distress
Darkened the watery diamond?

* In 1813.

THE EVIL HOUR

Such surge of black wings saw I never homing
Fast from a winter day's pale-gilt entombing
     Nor can the continent's entire woodland house them.
So many throats of known and unknown runnels
Shooting from thorny cliffs or poured through tunnels
     I never heard. Such rainstorm to arouse them
We in these parts yet bore not in such torrents,
Nor warring winds enraged so to abhorrence;
     The sun was laughed to scorn, his god-head pelted
With sharp bones wrenched from sylvan nature; flamed then
A lightning such, all other lightning (tamed then)
     Might be as honey or kind balms slow-melted.
Then this sad evening, this echo of existence,
And what was near driven to enormous distance.

from **EASTWARD** *(1950)*

MY ROOM

High up here I live
Right against the sky;
Pale and meditative
The moon comes here, and I.
Let folks ring below,
What do I care today?
It is no one that I know—
One being gone away.

Unseen by others here
I stitch each silken flower,
With inward tear on tear
Yet passionless: my tower
Gives me the cloudless sky.
From here I see the blue,
Star on star espy.
I see the tempest too.

96

Opposite my own
A chair stands through the hours.
His it was, that one;
One instant, it was ours.
There it stands, the chair,
A ribbon signing it,
As in a calm despair—
My case, placed opposite.

from the French of Marceline Deshordes-Valmore (1786-1859)

from **POEMS OF MANY YEARS** *(1957)*

YOUNG FIELDMOUSE

    Beseechingly this little thing—
Strayed from deep grass and breezy scented Spring
Into undreamed perils which have struck it down
Already—here in the den of the town
Takes refuge and finds pause in your warm palms
And dares to peer about, till its terror calms.

There is no hope for such a mangled mite,
Whose life depends on what we cannot guess,
Or nourishment or surgery; none the less
Indulge this child, this stranger with eye so bright,
So dim—so bright again, for love can do
Much, and the illusion is as good (in its time) as true.

We try our makeshifts, one by one they pass;
It tries; but in the end, in the long green grass,
The infant body stiffens, and the frame
Of the universe, to us, dies a little with the same.

THE FOND DREAM

Here's the dream I love.
    Stay, old Sleep, allow me this

Yet one moment, godlike bliss.
Here's the dream I love.

Tell us then that dream?
    O, it's nothing, nothing at all.
    But I was walking young and small
In a scene like a happy dream.

What especial scene?
    None especial: pure blue sky,
    Cherry orchards a brook runs by,
And an old church crowns the scene.

Only that? If so,
    All would be well; but, dreams have changed.
    Dreamers are banished, joys estranged.
I wake; it is not so.

C. E. B.
Ob. November 1951

Are all your eighty years defined at last
In so few terms? the chair and bookshelves by,
The latest pipe, the cared-for shoes, the stick
(Long since presented with some public thanks)
As good as new, but latterly less astir;
The post and railway times penned as of old
Beautifully for the fireside wall?
Not even your cricket-bag attending now,
Not the bream-ledger, nor the hopground picture,
Nor one school register, nor book of chants,
Though these will come to hand as days press on,
When your monastic face that seemed to pass
In a high procession from our local world,
Set on some boyhood vision, never uttered
To any but one, will be but village clay.

A HONG KONG HOUSE

'And now a dove and now a dragon-fly
Came to the garden; sometimes as we sat
Outdoors in twilight noiseless owl and bat
Flew shadowily by.
It was no garden,—so adust, red-dry
The rock-drift soil was, no kind root or sweet
Scent-subtle flower would house there, but I own
At certain seasons, burning bright,
Full-blown,
Some trumpet-purple blooms blazed at the sun's huge light.'

And then? tell more.
'The handy lizard and quite nimble toad
Had courage often to explore
Our large abode.
The infant lizard whipped across the wall
To his own objects; how to slide like him
Along the upright plane and never fall,
Ascribe to Eastern whim.
The winged ants flocked to our lamp, and shed
Their petally wings, and walked and crept instead.

'The palm-tree-top soared into the golden blue
And soaring skyward drew
Its straight stem etched with many rings,
And one broad holm-like tree whose name I never knew
Was decked through all its branches with broidering leaves
Of pattern-loving creepers; fine warblings
And gong-notes thence were sounded at our eaves
By clever birds one very seldom spied,
Except when they, of one tree tired,
Into another new-desired,
Over the lawn and playthings chose to glide.'

CHINESE PAPER-KNIFE

For the first time ever, and only now
   (Long waiting where I should see)
The tiny carved bird, the bony bough
   Start sharp into life for me.

Why not until now, why suddenly now
   This recognition? Replies
The bird must know who from that bough
   Holds me with staring eyes:

The owl once more, but this time found
   In foliage strange to me.
Fantastic branches warp around
   From the scaly uptwisting tree.

A trifle, ah yes: but the carver achieved
   A forest dream where flies
In and out the boughs so various-leaved
   This bird with the pinhead eyes.

Then praiséd be this to-day whose light
   Revealed this fabulous tree
And original owl, which many a night
   Will lead into mystery.

SUMMER STORM IN JAPANESE HILLS

This is the forecast storm, the rage
Of nature; mountain voices rise;
The lakes, it seems, would join the skies,
The winds begin an enterprise
Of scooping caves. This last brief stage,
Friend, of our journey! if our eyes
Can pierce this gray mass hissing past,
Or this strong road become not quite
A cataract shooting steep to night;
Or these swift wheels be just not whirled
As plaything chariots of the blast

Over the wan-hued tempest world
Where rock and tree like spindrift hurled
Will know as much as we at last.

THE STONE GARDEN (KYŌTO)

Signs and wonders fill
The air, the earth, and ocean
With tales of future triumph still,
And mansoul in commotion.

Let me like many others pause
By these mysterious forms of stone,
Which seem to speak eternal laws,
Truths which must not become unknown
At any point in time and space,
In boundless tides of startling hour and place,
Truths modest as these ancient quiet things
In this calm close (mere stones and sand it seems).
Elsewhere what fantasy of brief wonder springs:
Here see the soul which knows no wild extremes.

MILLSTREAM MEMORIES

Shattering remembrance, mercy! Not again
Could I delight in the child-bright scenes you wake.
Avoid, and quit my sight. Yet no: maintain
Whatever at last may guard me from the lake
Of darkness; dare not quit me,—stay, destroy
Some schemes and works which warped as time moved on;
Even the small pebble-songs bring rippling joy
Anew where later joy dropped woe-begone.
Gleam at my falling-off, assail my strength,
Deny my true love by far waters: she
Can understand, and all comes true at length,—
Your water-music teaches us to be.
I feared your elemental call, cool, light,
Leaf, life in the pearl? no more: shatter me quite.

LATER FLOWERS

'And still more later flowers'—*J. Keats*

Forgetful among his fancies, which once came to their best,
And sweetest tune long since the veteran will not rest;
Yet, blame not if perhaps among his closing hours
Sometimes a far-off moment may open long due flowers.

There was all abundance once, the field stretched to the sky
With blossom ablaze, some promises nevertheless lay by,
Until in the autumn morning, cool-lighted, one by one
They tint the still, grey spaces whence corn and poppies are gone.

AND AWAY

I sent her in fancy,
For the pastime of pursuing,
Wherever old Time had been
            Kind to me;
By snow-enchanted woodlands,
Valley orchards, river windings,
Ancient tracks through hill cornfields,
            Ahead smiled she.

I set her in fancy,
If I might go and greet her
By guildhalls and minsters,
By canal, by quay,
With hymns from glittering belfries,
With tunes from toying cafés,
Flower-markets, flower-costumes,
            Away explored she.

I thought she might laugh and
Rejoice, should I suddenly
Stand by her undecided
            In a far countree.
I was ghostly or dreaming,
Travelling all the long miles there.
I asked her to know me.
            'Elsewhere,' stared she.

DARKNESS

The fire dies down, and the last friend goes,
The vintage matters no more now;
Tomorrow's development no man knows,
But that we have faced before now;
    The night comes on apace.

Darkness. Our revels, if that name serves,
Are ended. Now for the battle of nerves.
The embers cool, the jokes turn sour,
The local's lost, and hugest power
    Comes prowling round the place.

But that's not new: there are older men
Who have been through that again and again—
There are children who will live to tell
The story of our stupid hell
    To a fresh and charming race,

For whom the night shall never need
Our smoky shelterings, day succeed
Unpresaged with our wilful moods
Transformed into enormous broods
    Of horror in dreadful chase.   early 1941

ANDREW MARVELL'S *HORTUS* TRANSLATED

What power so sways the hearts of human-kind
That with the laurel, palm, mere grass they bind
Their brows, and but one tree (almost) crowns all
Their conquering deeds?—such grudging coronal
Leaves temples bare. See, how together move
For Quiet's garlands, flowers to be inwove
Of every kind, and all the leafy grove.

Sweet spirit, Quiet, I clasp thee now, and thee,
Sister of Quiet, our Simplicity.

Through the great city, through the stately church,
The courts of Kings, long was, and vain, my search
For you; far thence in garden calm you stayed
Concealed in green plants and like-coloured shade.

Be mine into your fastnesses to stray,
Wearied, and drinking in a better day;
O leafy citizens, enfranchise me,
And of your flowering kingdom make me free!

Listening Apollo, and ye Muses, I
Loving not herds of men, nor Circus' cry,
Nor Forum's bellow, to Spring's shrine pursued
Unechoing honours, friendly solitude.

A maiden's beauty binds us all in spells,
Her snowy white your flourishing green excels,
And, I am sure, her rosy red o'erthrows;
Her locks yield to your leaves, her arms t' your boughs.
Your breezy whisper makes her voice less sweet.
But I have seen (and who could think to see 't?)
The cruel lover carve the mistress' name
Upon your finer skin, nor felt it shame
So to inscribe wounds on each sacred stem!
Should I, O trees, should I make bold with them,
Neaera, Chloe, will not there be named;
In her own book each tree shall be acclaimed.
Beloved Elm, Poplar and Cypress, Plane!
Faustina and Corinna, then adieu.

Love here, those weapons which so sharply flew
Let fall, the nerveless bow, the wings too doffed,
Puts slippers on, and saunters byways soft;
He lowers his torch; affrights no lover ever;
He lolls at ease, or dozes on his quiver;
Though Venus call, he will not hear: his dreams,
Not empty, shew the offence of former schemes.

The Immortals joy to see his lessening rage,
And though conversant through so many an age
With Nymphs and Goddesses, they all avow

Some tree gives each a better conquest now.
Jove for an old Oak pines and shuns his wife,
No rival so grieved Juno in her life;
No lover now invades poor Vulcan's bed,
The Beech drives Venus out of Mars's head;
Phoebus on lovely Daphne's steps has panted
That she might grow a Laurel, naught else wanted;
And did the goatfoot Pan for Syrinx speed,
'Twas but to own again his tuneful reed.

      *   *   *   *   *

Nor shall you, Gardener, modestly depart
Before my verse pays homage to your art;
With short-lived plants and ever pleasant flowers
You have marked the times of day and growing hours.
The clearer sun there rides through fragrant signs,
Nor in the angry Bull nor Crab's claw shines,
But slides to rose and violet's harmless sphere.
See, the bees too on honeyed work appear
To measure it with Thyme, their dial here.

O smoothly passing time, O gracious hours
Of peace told truly by your herbs and flowers.

A SWAN, A MAN

Among the dead reeds, the single swan
Floats and explores the water-shallow under,
While the wet whistling wind blows on
And the path by the river is all alone,
And I at the old bridge wonder
If those are birds or leaves,
Small quick birds or withered leaves,
Astir on the grassy patch of green
Where the wind is not so rough and keen.

What happens to my thought-time,
To my desires, my deeds, this day?

The rainstorm beats the pitiful stream
With battle-pictures I had hoped to miss,
But winter warfare could be worse than this;
Into the house, recall what dead friends say,
And like the Ancient Mariner learn to pray.   1964

'Festubert 1916' (page 32). Title altered to '1916 Seen from 1921' in *The Poems*, 1930.

'Eras' (page 44). Title altered to 'Achronos' in *English Poems*. Line 4 becomes 'Takes its new way already plain as though'; line 13 opens, 'Think . . .'.

'Zero' (page 49). Title altered to 'Come On, My Lucky Lads' in *Undertones*, which Blunden elsewhere noted as 'Worley's expression'; in the first stanza 'sky' is replaced by 'gloom' and 'dye' by 'bloom'. In *The Poems* the title reverts to 'Zero'.

'The Ancre at Hamel' (page 50). Title altered in *Undertones* to 'The Ancre at Hamel: Afterwards'.

'Winter: East Anglia' (page 52). The poem was first collected in *To Nature* under its original title, 'Winter Piece'. A later version has been chosen for reprinting because the earlier form is less powerful:
>   And, frost forgot, the chase grows hot
>   Till boys such spoil despise,
>   But the cornered weasel stands his ground,
>   Shrieks at the dogs and boys set round,
>   And like a fighter dies.

'The Midnight Skaters' (page 52). This was first collected in *Masks of Time*, where lines 3 and 4 (stanza 1) read: 'The pole-tops touch the star-gods' thrones/And sound the gulfs of wonder'. The version in the revised edition of *English Poems* (1929) is the familiar and stronger one.

'The Zonnebeke Road' (page 58). The impressive last line of this poem is an improvement on its original form in *Masks of Time*: 'And freeze you out with hate and save my brain'.

'To Joy' (page 70). Although this poem was first collected in *To Nature*, it was not until *The Poems* that Blunden removed the original, weakening archaisms: 'My blood away to give thee warm,/Thou ne'er on earth hast made one step,/. . . o'the storm.'